Write Your Own Texas Will (+CD-ROM)

Fourth Edition

Karen A. Rolcik and Mark Warda

Attorneys at Law

SPHINX® PUBLISHING
AN IMPRINT OF SOURCEBOOKS, INC.®
NAPERVILLE, ILLINOIS
www.SphinxLegal.com

D1292718

Fourth Edition: 2005

Published by: **Sphinx® Publishing, A Imprint of Sourcebooks, Inc.®**

<u>Naperville Office</u>
P.O. Box 4410
Naperville, Illinois 60567-4410
(630) 961-3900
Fax: 630-961-2168
www.sourcebooks.com
www.SphinxLegal.com

This publication is designed to provide accurate and authoritative information in regard to the subject matter covered. It is sold with the understanding that the publisher is not engaged in rendering legal, accounting, or other professional service. If legal advice or other expert assistance is required, the services of a competent professional person should be sought.

From a Declaration of Principles Jointly Adopted by a Committee of the American Bar Association and a Committee of Publishers and Associations

This product is not a substitute for legal advice.

Disclaimer required by Texas statutes.

Library of Congress Cataloging-in-Publication Data
Rolcik, Karen Ann.
 Write your own Texas will / Karen Ann Rolcik and Mark Warda.-- 4th ed.
    p. cm.
 Rev. ed. of: How to make a Texas will. 3rd ed. 2002.
 Includes index.
 ISBN 1-57248-513-2 (alk. paper)
 1. Wills--Texas--Popular works. 2. Inheritance and
succession--Texas--Popular works. 3. Wills--Texas--Forms. 4. Inheritance
and succession--Texas--Forms. I. Warda, Mark. II. Rolcik, Karen Ann. How to
make a Texas will. III. Title.

KFT1344.Z9R65 2005
346.76405'4--dc22   2005014617

Printed and bound in the United States of America.
BG — 10 9 8 7 6 5 4 3 2 1

Contents

How to Use the CD-ROM

Thank you for purchasing *Write Your Own Texas Will (+CD-ROM)*. We have included every document in the book on the CD-ROM that is attached to the inside back cover of the book.

You can use these forms just as you would the forms in the book. Print them out, fill them in, and use them however you need. You can also fill in the forms directly on your computer. Just identify the form you need, open it, click on the space where the information should go, and input your information. Customize each form for your particular needs. Use them over and over again.

The CD-ROM is compatible with both PC and Mac operating systems. (While it should work with either operating system, we cannot guarantee that it will work with your particular system and we cannot provide technical assistance.) To use the forms on your computer, you will need to use Adobe® Reader®. The CD-ROM does not contain this program. You can download this program from Adobe's website at **www.adobe.com**. Click on the "Get Adobe® Reader®" icon to begin the download process and follow the instructions.

Once you have Adobe® Reader® installed, insert the CD-ROM into your computer. Double click on the icon representing the disc on your desktop or go through your hard drive to identify the drive that contains the disc and click on it.

Once opened, you will see the files contained on the CD-ROM listed as "Form #: [Form Title]." Open the file you need through Adobe® Reader®. You may print the form to fill it out manually at this point, or your can use the "Hand Tool" and click on the appropriate line to fill it in using your computer.

Any time you see bracketed information [ ] on the form, you can click on it and delete the bracketed information from your final form. This information is only a reference guide to assist you in filling in the forms and should be removed from your final version. Once all your information is filled in, you can print your filled-in form.

NOTE: *Adobe® Reader® does not allow you to save the PDF with the boxes filled in.*

• • • • •

Purchasers of this book are granted a license to use the forms contained in it for their own personal use. By purchasing this book, you have also purchased a limited license to use all forms on the accompanying CD-ROM. The license limits you to personal use only and all other copyright laws must be adhered. No claim of copyright is made in any government form reproduced in the book or on the CD-ROM. You are free to modify the forms and tailor them to your specific situation.

The author and publisher have attempted to provide the most current and up-to-date information available. However, the courts, Congress, and your state's legislatures review, modify, and change laws on an ongoing basis, as well as create new laws from time to time. By the very nature of the information and due to the continual changes in our legal system, to be sure that you have the current and best information for your situation, you should consult a local attorney or research the current laws yourself.

• • • • •

This publication is designed to provide accurate and authoritative information in regard to the subject matter covered. It is sold with the understanding that the publisher is not engaged in rendering legal, accounting, or other professional service. If legal advice or other expert assistance is required, the services of a competent professional person should be sought.

> —*From a Declaration of Principles Jointly Adopted by a Committee of the American Bar Association and a Committee of Publishers and Associations*

This product is not a substitute for legal advice.

> —*Disclaimer required by Texas statutes*

Using Self-Help Law Books

Before using a self-help law book, you should realize the advantages and disadvantages of doing your own legal work and understand the challenges and diligence that this requires.

The Growing Trend

Rest assured that you will not be the first or only person handling your own legal matter. For example, in some states, more than 75% of the people in divorces and other cases represent themselves. Because of the high cost of legal services, this is a major trend and many courts are struggling to make it easier for people to represent themselves. However, some courts are not happy with people who do not use attorneys and refuse to help them in any way. For some, the attitude is, "Go to the law library and figure it out for yourself."

We write and publish self-help law books to give people an alternative to the often complicated and confusing legal books found in most law libraries. We have made the explanations of the law as simple and easy to understand as possible. Of course, unlike an attorney advising an individual client, we cannot cover every conceivable possibility.

Cost/Value Analysis

Whenever you shop for a product or service, you are faced with various levels of quality and price. In deciding what product or service to buy, you make a cost/value analysis on the basis of your willingness to pay and the quality you desire.

When buying a car, you decide whether you want transportation, comfort, status, or sex appeal. Accordingly, you decide among such choices as a Neon, a Lincoln, a Rolls Royce, or a Porsche. Before making a decision, you usually weigh the merits of each option against the cost.

When you get a headache, you can take a pain reliever (such as aspirin) or visit a medical specialist for a neurological examination. Given this choice, most people, of course, take a pain reliever, since it costs only pennies; whereas a medical examination costs hundreds of dollars and takes a lot of time. This is usually a logical choice because it is rare to need anything more than a pain reliever for a headache. But in some cases, a headache may indicate a brain tumor and failing to see a specialist right away can result in complications. Should everyone with a headache go to a specialist? Of course not, but people treating their own illnesses must realize that they are betting on the basis of their cost/value analysis of the situation. They are taking the most logical option.

The same cost/value analysis must be made when deciding to do one's own legal work. Many legal situations are very straight forward, requiring a simple form and no complicated analysis. Anyone with a little intelligence and a book of instructions can handle the matter without outside help.

But there is always the chance that complications are involved that only an attorney would notice. To simplify the law into a book like this, several legal cases often must be condensed into a single sentence or paragraph. Otherwise, the book would be several hundred pages long and too complicated for most people. However, this simplification necessarily leaves out many details and nuances that would apply to special or unusual situations. Also, there are many ways to interpret most legal questions. Your case may come before a judge who disagrees with the analysis of our authors.

Therefore, in deciding to use a self-help law book and to do your own legal work, you must realize that you are making a cost/value analysis. You have decided that the money you will save in doing it yourself outweighs the chance that your case will not turn out to your satisfaction. Most people handling their own simple legal matters never have a problem, but occasionally people find that it ended up costing them more to have an attorney straighten out the situation than it would have if they had hired an attorney in the beginning. Keep this in mind while handling your case, and be sure to consult an attorney if you feel you might need further guidance.

Local Rules   The next thing to remember is that a book which covers the law for the entire nation, or even for an entire state, cannot possibly include every procedural difference of every jurisdiction. Whenever possible, we provide the exact form needed; however, in some areas, each county, or even each judge, may require unique forms and procedures. In our state books, our forms usually cover the majority of counties in the state, or provide examples of the type of form which will be required. In our national books, our forms are sometimes even more general in nature but are designed to give a good idea of the type of form that will be needed in most locations. Nonetheless, keep in mind that your state, county, or judge may have a requirement or use a form that is not included in this book.

You should not necessarily expect to be able to get all of the information and resources you need solely from within the pages of this book. This book will serve as your guide, giving you specific information whenever possible and helping you to find out what else you will need to know. This is just like if you decided to build your own backyard deck. You might purchase a book on how to build decks. However, such a book would not include the building codes and permit requirements of every city, town, county, and township in the nation; nor would it include the lumber, nails, saws, hammers, and other materials and tools you would need to actually build the deck. You would use the book as your guide, and then do some work and research involving such matters as whether you need a permit of some kind, what type and grade of wood are available in your area, whether to use hand tools or power tools, and how to use those tools.

Before using the forms in a book like this, you should check with your court clerk to see if there are any local rules of which you should be aware, or local forms you will need to use. Often, such forms will require the same information as the forms in the book but are merely laid out differently or use slightly different language. They will some-times require additional information.

Changes in the Law

Besides being subject to local rules and practices, the law is subject to change at any time. The courts and the legislatures of all fifty states are constantly revising the laws. It is possible that while you are reading this book, some aspect of the law is being changed.

In most cases, the change will be of minimal significance. A form will be redesigned, additional information will be required, or a waiting period will be extended. As a result, you might need to revise a form, file an extra form, or wait out a longer time period; these types of changes will not usually affect the outcome of your case. On the other hand, sometimes a major part of the law is changed, the entire law in a particular area is rewritten, or a case that was the basis of a cen-tral legal point is overruled. In such instances, your entire ability to pursue your case may be impaired.

Again, you should weigh the value of your case against the cost of an attorney and make a decision as to what you believe is in your best interest.This book is written to help Texas residents quickly and easily make their own wills without the expense or delay of hiring a lawyer. It begins with a short explanation of how a will works and what a will can and cannot do. It is designed to allow those with simple estates to quickly and inexpensively set up their affairs to distribute their prop-erty according to their wishes. It also includes an explanation of how such things as joint property, pay on death accounts, life insurance, and retirement plans will affect your planning.

Introduction

This book is written to help Texas residents quickly and easily make their own wills without the expense or delay of hiring a lawyer. Chapter 1 begins with a short explanation of how a will works and what a will can and cannot do. It is designed to allow those with simple estates to quickly and inexpensively set up their affairs to distribute their property according to their wishes. This book also includes an explanation of how things such as joint property, pay on death accounts, life insurance, and retirement plans will affect your planning.

In addition, this book includes information on how to appoint a guardian for any minor children you may have. This helps avoid bad feelings and arguments between relatives, and can protect your children from being raised by someone you would object to.

Chapters 1 through 10 have basic explanations of the laws that affect the making of a will and the process of making your own will and other estate planning documents. Appendix A contains some of the actual statutes governing wills and probate. Appendix B contains information regarding federal and Texas estate taxes. Appendix C contains sample filled-in forms to show you how it is done. Appendix D contains blank forms you can use. A flow chart in Appendix D will help you choose the right will form based upon your circumstances and desires. All same forms are also on the CD-ROM attached to the back cover of the book.

You can prepare your own will quickly and easily by using the forms in this book. You can use the original blank forms in Appendix D, photocopy them, or print a copy from the CD-ROM. You can also fill in all the information on the form directly from your computer. The small amount of time you take to do this can give you and your loved ones peace of mind knowing that your estate will be distributed according to your wishes.

Before using any of the forms in Appendix D, you should read and understand all of the information in this book. A surprising number of people have had their estates pass to the wrong persons because of a simple lack of knowledge of how the laws work.

In each example given in the text you might ask, "What if the spouse died first?" or "What if the children were grown up?" and the solution might change because of your question. If your situation is complicated, you should seek the advice of an attorney. In many communities, wills are available for very reasonable prices. No book of this type can cover every contingency in every case, but a knowledge of the basics will help you to make the right decisions regarding your property.

The forms in this book are designed to leave property to your family, or if you have no family, to friends or charities. As explained in Chapter 3, if you wish to disinherit your family and leave your property to others, you should consult with an attorney who can be sure that your will cannot be successfully challenged in court.

The Basics about Wills

A *will* is a document that can be used to control who gets your property after your death, who will be the guardian of your minor children and control the property that you leave to your children, and who will manage your estate upon your death.

A will becomes effective *only* after your death. When you sign a will in accordance with Texas laws, it is *valid*. But it does not become effective until after you die. Many people think that a power of attorney can be used to give your property away after you die. This is not true. A power of attorney dies with you. That is, when you die, the power of attorney is no longer effective.

Before making your will, you should understand how a will works and what a will can and cannot do. If you do not understand these things, your wishes may not be carried out and people you do not intend may end up with your property.

HOW A WILL WORKS

A will serves a number of different purposes. Each purpose is important and depending on your particular circumstances, having a will can be crucial.

The most obvious role of your will is to direct the disposition of your property after your death. You can give specific gifts of personal items to individuals, make specific *bequests* (or gifts) of money to individuals, and allocate the balance of your assets among individuals in varying percentages. You can also leave gifts to churches, schools, and charities.

Without a will, you have no control over who will receive your property and how much they will receive. If you do not have a will, who your beneficiaries will be and the share of your property to which they are entitled is established by Texas law—not your wishes.

Texas calls the person who represents your estate and handles the probate process the *executor*. An executor is the person who gathers together all of your assets and distributes them to the beneficiaries. A will allows you to decide who will be the executor of your estate. If you do not name an executor in your will or if you do not have a will, the executor of your estate will be appointed by the court. Texas has a statute that establishes who can be appointed as executor and in what order. While family members are generally favored under the statutes, it is possible that an unrelated person, a bank or trust company, or even a creditor of your estate can be appointed executor of your estate.

With a will, you can provide that your executor does not have to post a surety bond with the court in order to serve. This can save the estate a sizeable amount of money. The executor can also be granted broad powers in addition to the powers given to executors by law to handle estate matters. If you own a business, you can designate that the executor has full authority to operate the business without posting a bond or employing a professional business advisor.

Perhaps one of the most overlooked purposes of a will is the designation of a *guardian* for minor children. In a will, you can designate who will be entrusted with the care and upbringing of your children. This way, you can avoid fights among relatives and make sure that the person who is most familiar with you and your children will raise them. If you do not appoint a guardian for your minor children, Texas law designates who will be eligible to be appointed guardian. Often to assist the court with this determination, a social study will be conducted by the child services department to evaluate who is best-suited to raise your children.

Many people have definite ideas about who they want to raise their minor children but are not confident in the guardian's ability to manage the children's inheritance. In your will, you can also designate a person to act as guardian of the children's financial inheritance.

Finally, and perhaps most importantly, a Texas will can direct that your estate be administered in accordance with simplified probate procedures. This is called an *independent estate administration*.

YOUR WILL AND PROBATE

Some people think that a will avoids the *probate* process when in fact it does not. A will is the document used in the probate process to determine who receives the property, who is appointed to be guardian of minor children, and who is appointed to act as executor of the estate.

Probate is the legal process by which property in an estate is transferred to the *heirs* and *beneficiaries* of a deceased person (the *decedent*). Heirs are persons who are entitled to receive a decedent's property if the decedent dies without a will. Beneficiaries are persons who are named in a decedent's will to receive property.

The probate process begins by presenting the will of the decedent to the judge or, if there is no will, by presenting a list of the decedent's property and a list of the people to whom it is proposed that the property be given. The probate process is discussed in greater detail in Chapter 2.

PROPERTY THAT PASSES BY WILL

Property that is in the name of a person will be transferred under the terms of the person's will unless it falls within certain exceptions. These exceptions are described later in the section titled "Avoiding Probate."

In addition to property in the name of one person alone, there are several other types of property owned by a person that will be transferred under the terms of a will. These types of property include *tenancy in common*, *community property*, *homestead property*, and *exempt property*.

Tenancy in Common

There are two basic ways to own property with another person—joint tenancy with right of survivorship and tenancy in common. Joint tenancy with right of survivorship property is discussed later in this Chapter. *Tenancy in common* means that one or more persons own property together—all of their names are on the title to the property. When one owner dies, that owner's share of the property will be given to his or her heirs or beneficiaries named in the owner's will. The other owners do *not* get the decedent's share of the property unless they are named as beneficiaries in the decedent's will. People use tenancy in common if they do not want the co-owner to inherit their share of the property when they die.

Tenancy in common property is owned by each of the owners. One owner cannot withdraw his or her contribution or sell the property without the approval of the other owners. At times, this can cause problems because if an emergency arises, an owner cannot use his or her share of the tenancy in common property without the other owners' consent.

Example 1:
Tom and Marcia bought a house and lived together for twenty years but were never married. The deed to the house had both of their names on it. Tom and Marcia contributed equally to the purchase of the home. Tom's will leaves all of his property to his brother. Tom believed that because Marcia's name was on the deed she would become the sole owner of the house upon his death. When Tom died, his brother received all of his property including Tom's one-half interest in the house. Because Marcia could not afford to buy Tom's share of the house from his brother, the house had to be sold.

Example 2:
Bob and Joy, brother and sister, opened a bank account together. They both deposited money into the account.

Bob has emergency medical bills and needs to use his money in the account to pay those bills. Because both of their names are on the account, the bank will not let either one of them withdraw money without the signature or approval of the other owner.

Community and Separate Property

Under Texas law, property possessed by either spouse during a marriage is classified as *community property* or *separate property*. Separate property is property owned by a spouse before the marriage, property acquired during the marriage by gift or inheritance, and funds received by a spouse for personal injuries. All other property acquired during the marriage is community property.

Each spouse is considered to own a one-half interest in the community property. A spouse owns 100% of his or her separate property and his or her will controls 100% of the separate property. When a spouse dies, his or her will controls only that spouse's one-half interest in the community property. The surviving spouse is entitled to keep his or her one-half interest in the community property.

Example 1:

Mark and Barb have been married for several years. During their marriage, Barb stayed at home to raise the children. Their stocks and bank accounts are only in Mark's name. Mark's will leaves all of his property to his sister, Liz, and nothing to his wife. Barb gets one-half of all property that the court designates as *community property*. Mark's sister gets the other half of the property and all of Mark's separate property, if Mark has any separate property.

Example 2:

Bill and Jane are married and both work. Prior to their marriage, Jane saved $5,000 and kept this property in a separate account. While they are married, Jane's parents die leaving her $20,000. Jane's will leaves all of her property to her brother, Derk. Derk gets the $25,000 of the separate property (the bank account and Jane's inheritance from parents) and Jane's one-half of any community property Jane and Bill accumulated during their marriage.

A provision unique to Texas community property law is that the income earned by a spouse's separate property is considered community property. Therefore, in Example 2, suppose Jane's separate property account earned $5,000 income during the marriage. At Jane's death, Derk gets one-half of the income and Bill gets the other half.

Homestead Property

Under Texas law, the term *homestead* has two meanings. In one sense, homestead refers to the reduction in property taxes that you get from the county tax assessor when you reside on the property and use it as your primary residence. In another sense, homestead means the property that is the permanent residence of a legal resident of Texas and is therefore entitled to certain protections and restrictions under Texas law.

If your property is homestead in the second sense, your will cannot destroy the rights of your surviving spouse and minor children in the homestead. Your surviving spouse has the right to live in the homestead for the rest of his or her life, no matter who you give it to under your will. Upon the surviving spouse's death, or when the surviving spouse no longer uses the property as a homestead, the homestead passes to the beneficiaries named in your will.

If you have minor children but no spouse, the children have the right to live in the homestead for as long as necessary while they are minors. After a court determines that it is no longer necessary to use the homestead for your children, or when your children reach age 18, the homestead passes to the people named in your will.

Example 1:
John and Dawn are married. John has adult children from a prior marriage. John's will leaves his house (which is his homestead) to his adult children and the rest of his property to his wife, Dawn. Upon his death, Dawn gets all of the property and has the right to live

in the house for the rest of her life or until she moves to another house. Upon her death or when she moves, John's children get the house even though Dawn's will leaves all of her property to her brother.

Example 2:

Margaret is a widow with two minor children. In her will, she leaves her homestead to her parents and the rest of her property to her children. The children have the right to use the homestead until they reach age 18 or are able to support themselves. When both of the children are able to support themselves, Margaret's parents get the homestead.

Exempt Property

If you have a spouse or minor children, then up to $30,000 in household furniture, furnishings, and appliances in your usual place of abode (residence) and all automobiles in your name that are regularly used by you or members of your family are not bound by the terms of your will. This property is called *exempt property*. If you have a spouse, your spouse gets this property. If you have no spouse but have minor children, your children receive the exempt property. Additionally, a spouse and minor children may receive a *family allowance* of an amount deemed reasonable by a court to defray living expenses during the first year following the death.

Example:

Donna dies and her will gives half her property to her husband, David, and half to her grown son from a prior marriage. Donna's property consists of a $5,000 automobile, $5,000 in furniture, and $5,000 in cash. Donna's husband may be able to get the car and the furniture as exempt property and the $5,000 as a family allowance, leaving nothing for her son.

AVOIDING PROBATE

If you wish to transfer your property and avoid the probate process at your death, you must use methods to transfer property other than a will. These methods include joint tenancy, pay on death accounts (POD accounts) or I/T/F accounts ("In Trust For"), beneficiary designations, and trusts. These methods are briefly discussed.

If a person successfully avoids probate with all of his or her property, then he or she may not need a will. In many cases, when a husband or wife dies, no will or probate is necessary because everything is jointly owned. However, everyone should have a will in case someone forgets to put some property into joint ownership or in case both husband and wife die in the same accident.

Joint Tenancy

Property that is owned in *joint tenancy with right of survivorship* does not pass through a will and does not go through the probate process. Joint tenancy property is usually owned by at least two people who are called *joint tenants*. When one joint owner dies, the joint tenancy property automatically passes to the remaining owner. In many cases, the name of the deceased joint owner can be removed from title to joint tenancy property by simply providing a death certificate. Joint tenancy overrides the terms of a person's will.

However, there are exceptions to the general rule that joint tenancy property avoids probate. If money is put into a joint account only for convenience and the parties intend that the property should pass under the terms of the will, the money might pass through the will. But if the joint owner refuses to give the money to the estate of the deceased person, it could take an expensive court battle to get the money back.

Putting property into joint tenancy does not give the joint owner absolute rights to the property. If the decedent's estate owes federal or Texas estate taxes, the surviving joint owner may have to give up some of the joint tenancy property to make the estate tax payments. Also, if property is determined to be *community property*, part or all of the property may pass to the surviving spouse rather than the joint owner.

Example 1:

Ted and his wife, Michelle, want all of their property to go to each other if one dies before the other. They put their house, cars, bank accounts, and investment accounts into joint ownership. When Ted dies, Michelle only has to show his death certificate to the banks, county clerk, and investment companies to get the property transferred into her name alone. No probate or will is necessary.

Example 2:

After Ted's death, Michelle puts all of the property and accounts into joint ownership with her son, Mark. Upon Michelle's death, Mark needs only to present her death certificate to have everything transferred into his name. No probate or will is necessary.

Joint tenancy and your will. Complications can arise when some property is held in joint tenancy and some property passes through a will. In such a case, a person's plans about the distribution of his property may not be fulfilled.

Example 1:

Bill's will leaves all of his property to his sister, Mary, who is disabled. Bill dies owning a house jointly with his wife, Joan, and a bank account jointly with his son, Don. Upon Bill's death, Joan gets the house, Don gets the bank account, and Mary gets nothing.

Example 2:

Betty's will leaves half of her assets to her sister, Ann, and half of her assets to her husband, George. Betty dies owning $1,000,000 in stock jointly with George and a car in her name alone. Ann gets only a half interest in the car. George gets all of the stock and a half interest in the car.

Example 3:

John's will leaves all of his property equally to his five children. Before going into the hospital, John puts his oldest son, Harry, as a joint owner of his accounts to manage them while he recuperates. John dies and Harry gets all of his assets. The rest of the children get nothing.

In each of the previous examples, the property went to a person it probably should not have because the decedent did not realize that joint ownership overruled his or her will. In some families, this might not be a problem. Harry might share the property equally with the rest of the children. But Harry might also keep everything, and the family would never talk to him again or would take him to court.

NOTE: *On a bank account, joint tenancy and joint property are commonly designated with the word "OR" (e.g., Bob or Mary Smith). Property to be titled as tenants in common is commonly designated with the word "AND" (e.g., Bob and Mary Smith). Under joint tenancy, the other owner takes it all at the death of the other. Under the tenants in common, one-half of the property is owned by the decedent and the rest of the property is owned by the joint owner. Upon the decedent's death, his or her one-half of the property would pass under his or her will.*

Risks of joint tenancy. In many cases, joint property can be an ideal way to own property and avoid probate. However, it does have risks. If you put your real estate into joint ownership with someone, you cannot sell it or mortgage it without the other person's signature. If you put your bank account into joint tenancy with someone else, he or she can withdraw all of the money from the bank account even though none of the money was his or hers.

Example 1:

Alice puts her house into joint ownership with her son, Tom. She later marries Ed and moves in with him. She wanted to sell her house and invest the money to generate income. Her son refuses to sign the deed to sell the house because he wanted to keep the home in the family. Alice had to go to court to sue her son to get her house back. (The judge could have refused to give Alice her house back.)

Example 2:

Alex put his bank accounts into joint ownership with his daughter, Mary, to avoid probate. Mary fell in love with Doug who was in trouble with the law. Doug talked Mary into "borrowing" $30,000 from the account for business deals that went sour. Later, Mary "borrowed" $25,000 more to pay Doug's bail bond. Alex did not find out about the amounts Mary borrowed until it was too late and his money was gone.

Pay on Death Accounts

It is possible to designate a bank account as a *pay on death* (POD) account. These accounts can also be known as *in trust for* (I/T/F) accounts. The name on the account remains the same but the bank is instructed to transfer the money in the account upon the death of the owner to the person the owner has designated. In essence, a pay on death account has a beneficiary designation like a life insurance policy. The person who is named to receive the POD account has no right to any money in the account while the owner of the account is alive. A will does not control the distribution of the POD account, so POD accounts do not pass through probate.

Example:

Robert has a bank account that he wants to go to his granddaughter when he dies. Robert designates his granddaughter as the beneficiary of the POD bank account. When Robert dies, his granddaughter receives the bank account automatically. Prior to Robert's death, his granddaughter has no control over the account and has no access to the account. In fact, she does not even have to know about the account. Robert can take his granddaughter's name off the account at any time.

Beneficiary Designations   Assets such as life insurance policies, annuities, and retirement plans require that the owner of the assets name one or more persons to receive the policy, annuity, or retirement plan when the owner dies. The owner must sign a beneficiary designation form that names who will receive the asset. If more than one person is named as a beneficiary, the beneficiary designation form will also state how much each beneficiary will receive. Often, this is expressed in the form of a certain percentage of the asset.

Example:

Mike has a life insurance policy. He wants his three children to receive the payout from the life insurance policy after his death. On a beneficiary form, Mike designates each child by name and that each child is to receive an equal share. During his lifetime, Mike can change the beneficiaries at any time.

Assets that pass by beneficiary designation do not pass through the probate process. A will has no effect on the distribution of such assets.

Example:

Judith has a retirement plan and a will. She wants to give all of her assets to her mother when she dies. The only asset that Judith owns other than the retirement plan is her car. The beneficiary designation for the retirement plan names her daughter as beneficiary. Judith's will names her mother as sole beneficiary of her estate. When Judith dies, her daughter gets the retirement plan and her mother gets the car.

Trusts   A very popular way to avoid probate is to use a *trust*. The trust is a contract between the *maker* of the trust, the *trustee*, and the *beneficiaries*. A trust is created when an individual signs a legal document, a trust agreement, which contains certain provisions. The trust agreement contains the terms of the contract—the rights, duties, and obligations of the maker of the trust and the person who controls the trust, the trustee.

Living Trust   A trust is an arrangement for the ownership of property. When the maker of the trust transfers property to a trust, legal title to the assets is vested in the trustee. Because the trust is now the owner of the property, when the maker of the trust dies, the property passes to the beneficiaries designated in the trust agreement without going through the probate process.

A trust created during the lifetime of the maker of the trust (the person who owns the property) that is effective while the maker is living has commonly been called a *living trust*. In most living trusts, the maker of the trust is the beneficiary of the trust throughout his or her lifetime and is generally the trustee responsible for the management and distribution of trust assets. The beneficiaries who will receive the trust property when the maker dies have no control over or rights to the trust property until the maker dies.

Example:

Jim creates a trust to own property while he is alive. Jim controls the trust during his lifetime. He has named his children as beneficiaries of his trust after his death. When Jim dies, the property in the trust passes directly to his children in accordance with the terms of the trust agreement. Jim's will does not control the distribution of the trust property.

PAYMENT OF DEBTS AND EXPENSES

In addition to directing the distribution of property, a will also directs that a person's debts, funeral expenses, and final medical expenses be paid. One of the duties of the person administering the estate (the *executor*) is to pay the debts of the decedent. Before the property of an estate can be distributed to the beneficiaries named in the will, the legitimate debts of the decedent, the funeral expenses, and the expenses of the last illness must be identified and paid.

An exception to this general rule applies to *secured debts*. Secured debts are protected by a lien on specific property. Common examples of secured debts are home loans and car loans. In the case of a secured debt, the loan does not necessarily have to be paid before the property is distributed.

Example:

John owns a $100,000 house with an $80,000 mortgage and he has $100,000 in the bank. If he leaves the house to his brother and the bank account to his sister, then his brother receives the home but owes the $80,000 mortgage.

A person can include a provision in his or her will that requires that a secured debt be paid with other assets of the estate. In the previous example, if John included a provision in his will that the mortgage be paid with estate assets, his brother would receive the house and his sister would receive only $20,000 after $80,000 is used to pay the mortgage.

What if your debts are more than your property? Today, unlike hundreds of years ago, people cannot inherit other people's debts. A person's property must first be used to pay funeral expenses, expenses of the last illness, and expenses of probate. If there is no money left over, other creditors are out of luck. However, if a person leaves property to someone and there is not enough cash to pay his or her debts, then the property will be sold to raise money to pay the debts.

Example:

Jeb's will leaves all of his property to his three children. At the time of his death, Jeb has $30,000 in medical bills and $11,000 in credit card debt. The only assets are his car and $5,000 in stock. The car and stock are sold to pay the funeral bill and probate fees are paid out of the proceeds of the sale of stock. If any money is left, it goes to the creditors and nothing is left for the children. The children do not have to use their own money to pay the medical bills or credit card debt.

chapter 2

The Probate Process

As stated in Chapter 1, *probate* is the legal process by which property in an estate is transferred to the heirs and beneficiaries of a deceased person (the *decedent*). The will is the primary document used in the probate process. A will does not eliminate the need for probate. Probate may be necessary whether or not a decedent had a will. Probate is required if the decedent owned property in his or her individual name at the time of his or her death.

If a decedent died without signing a will, then the decedent died *intestate* and his or her property will pass to his or her *heirs at law*. The Texas Probate Code lists the heirs of a decedent, the order in which they will inherit from the decedent, and the amount of that inheritance. In effect, Texas has written a will for the decedent and dictates who will receive the property without regard to the wishes of the decedent, or the true needs of the decedent's family situation. If no living relative of the decedent can be located, all of the decedent's property *escheats* to the State. That is, the State of Texas is the beneficiary of the decedent's entire estate.

In general, if a person dies without a will, Texas law provides for distribution of the assets *down the family tree*. If the person dies and leaves a surviving spouse, a significant portion, if not all of the assets, will go to the surviving spouse. If there is no surviving spouse, the assets go to children or grandchildren. If there are minor children, assets may be set aside to be distributed to them upon the attainment of age 18. If there is no surviving spouse, children, or grandchildren, the assets are distributed to parents, and then brothers and sisters of the decedent.

If a decedent died with a signed will, then the decedent died *testate* and his or her property passes to the individuals named in his or her will, the *beneficiaries*. If a person challenges the validity of the decedent's will, often called *contesting the will*, the probate court will get involved in determining whether the beneficiaries named in the decedent's will are legally entitled to receive the property.

ADMINISTRATION OF THE ESTATE

Administering the estate refers to the process undertaken by the executor of the estate to collect and value the property of the estate; pay debts, expenses, and taxes; and, distribute the remaining property to the beneficiaries.

Texas has a statute that permits a person to direct that his or her estate be administered on an expedited basis. Certain language must be included in the will that permits the estate to be administered *independent* of court supervision. Most wills in Texas contain the language that permits an independent administration of the estate.

The following is a fairly representative outline of the Texas probate process and how an estate is administered.

- ✪ A *petition* or *application* is filed with the probate court either asking that a will be admitted to probate, or stating that a person died without leaving a will.

- ✪ A hearing is held in which the testimony of a family member, executor, or witness to the will is presented to the court to establish proof of death, proof of the will, or, if the person died without a will, proof of the heirs of the decedent.

✪ If there is a will, an order is signed acknowledging the will, and some type of document is issued by the court giving the personal representative power to act for the estate. This may be called *Letters of Administration* or *Letters Testamentary*.

✪ If there is no will, the court will issue some type of document identifying the heirs of the decedent according to the Texas statutes of descent and distribution. This may be called *Letters of Administration*.

✪ If there is no will, the court will appoint a person to act as administrator for the estate. The duties of the administrator are similar to that of an executor.

✪ Creditors are notified to permit them to file claims against the estate.

✪ The executor must collect all of the assets of the decedent and appraise the assets to obtain a current fair market value.

✪ The executor must pay the debts of the decedent and the expenses of the estate administration, including attorney, accountant, and appraiser fees; probate costs; and, the like.

✪ If the value of the estate is in excess of $1,500,000, the executor must prepare and file a federal estate tax return and Texas estate tax return within nine months of the decedent's death. If federal or Texas estate taxes are due, the tax must be paid when the estate tax return is filed.

✪ The executor distributes remaining assets to the beneficiaries named in the will or if there is no will, to the heirs by law.

In Texas, the probate process can often be completed in as little as six months. The probate process can be made easier if you include clear instructions in your will about who should serve as executor, guardian of minor children, and who will receive your property. In addition, if you leave organized information about your property and debts, much time will be saved because the executor will not have to spend time locating such information.

The Need for a Will

Many people put off making a will because they are not comfortable with discussing their death and what will happen when they are dead. Other reasons people do not make a will are because they think that they do not have enough property to make a will or because they mistakenly believe that all of their property will go to their spouse or children automatically when they die. Finally, many people delay making a will because they simply cannot decide who to name as executor or guardian of their minor children or who they want to get their property.

It is important to remember that wills can be changed as many times as a person would like. A will is not written in stone. It is very important that a person write a will even if he or she cannot make a final decision on issues such as appointing an executor or guardian. You can write a will and go back and change it when final decisions are made. Procrastination is not an option.

WHAT A WILL CAN DO

A will allows you to decide who will be a *beneficiary*—a person who inherits your property after your death. You can give specific personal items to certain persons and choose which people, if any, deserve a greater share of your estate. You can also leave gifts to schools and charities.

A will allows you to designate an *executor*—the person who will be in charge of handling your estate. This person gathers all your assets and distributes them to the beneficiaries, pays any debts you owe at the time of your death, hires attorneys or accountants if necessary, and files any essential tax or probate forms. You can provide in a will that your executor does not have to post a *surety bond* with the court in order to serve, which can save your estate some money. You can also give the executor the power to sell your property and take other actions without a court order.

A will allows you to choose a *guardian*—a person to raise your minor children. By designating a guardian, you can avoid fights among relatives about who will raise your children. You may also appoint separate guardians over your children and their money. For example, you may appoint your sister as guardian over your children and your father as guardian over their money. That way, a second person can provide input on how the children's money is spent.

Protecting Heirs

Beyond naming the people to benefit and manage your estate, a will can also direct how the process will be handled and how to maximize what you can pass on. You can set up a *trust* to provide that your property is not distributed immediately. Many people feel that their children would not be ready to handle large sums of money at the *age of majority*, which is age 18. A will can direct the money to be held in a trust until the children are 21, 25, or older.

Minimizing Taxes

If your estate is over the amount protected by the federal *unified credit* ($1,500,000, but will be phased out completely by the year 2010), then it will be subject to federal estate taxes. If you wish to lower those taxes by making gifts to charities, for example, you can do so through a will. However, such estate planning is beyond the scope of this book and you should consult an estate planning attorney or another book for further information.

Independent Estate Administration

By including special language in your will, you can provide that your executor is an *independent executor,* which means he or she can administer your estate independent of court supervision. This saves a great deal of time and money because it frees your executor from filing lots of paperwork with the court and from having to first obtain the court's permission before handling estate matters as they arise.

If the special language designating your executor as an independent executor is not included in your will, your executor will be a *dependent executor.* A dependent executor must make frequent reports to the court and is often required to obtain permission from the court prior to taking certain acts. For instance, a dependent executor may have to obtain the permission of the court to sell assets to pay debts, expenses, or taxes, and to make distributions to the beneficiaries named in your will. Dependent administrations can be very time consuming and expensive.

DYING WITHOUT A WILL

If you do not have a will, Texas law dictates how your property will be distributed. The law will distinguish between separate and community property and distribute your property as follows.

- ✪ If you leave a spouse and no children, your spouse gets all of your separate personal property, all of your community property, and half of your separate real property. The other half of the real property goes to either your parents, your brothers and sisters (or their children), your grandparents, or your aunts and uncles (or their children).

- ✪ If you leave a spouse and children, your spouse gets ownership of half of all community property and one-third of your separate personal property. Your children get ownership of half of all community property, two-thirds of your separate personal property, and all of your separate real property. Your spouse has the right, however, to share the benefits from one-third of your separate real property. (These benefits commonly are the right to live on the property.)

✪ If you leave children and no spouse, all of your children get equal shares of your estate.

✪ If you leave no spouse *and* no children, then your estate goes to the living people highest on the following list:

- your parents;

- your brothers and sisters (or if dead, their children);

- your grandparents; and,

- your uncles and aunts or their children.

OUT-OF-STATE WILLS

A will that is valid in another state is probably valid to pass property in Texas. However, before such a will can be accepted by a Texas Probate Court, a person in your former state has to be appointed as a *foreign executor*. The role of the foreign executor is to locate a person who witnessed your signature on the will and take the oath of that witness that the will was validly executed. Because of the expense and delay of having a foreign executor appointed and the problem of finding out-of-state witnesses, it is advised that you execute a new will after moving to Texas.

Another advantage to having a Texas will is that, as a Texas resident, your estate will pay no state probate or inheritance taxes. If you move to Texas but keep your old will, your former state of residence may try to collect taxes on your estate by claiming that you are still a resident of that state.

Example:
George and Barbara left their high-tax state and retired to Texas, but they never made a new will. Upon their

deaths, their former state of residence tried to collect a tax from their estate because their wills stated that they were residents of that state.

Texas also allows a will to be *self-proved,* which means that witnesses never have to be called to court to take an oath and give testimony. With special self-proving language in your will, the witnesses take an oath at the time of signing and never have to be seen again. Also, a Texas will allows you to make your executor an *independent executor* saving your estate a lot of time and expense.

WHO CAN MAKE A TEXAS WILL

Any person who is 18 years of age and of sound mind can make a valid will in Texas.

WHAT A WILL CANNOT DO

A will cannot direct that anything illegal be done, and it cannot put unreasonable conditions on a gift. For example, a provision that your daughter receives all of your property if she divorces her husband would be ignored by the court. She would get the property with no conditions attached. You can put some conditions in your will, but be sure they are enforceable by consulting an attorney.

A will cannot leave money or property to an animal because animals cannot legally own property. If you wish to continue paying for the care of an animal after your death, you should leave the funds in a trust or to a friend whom you know will care for the animal.

WHEN NOT TO USE A SIMPLE WILL

Absolutely anyone can use a simple will. No matter what your situation, you can use the wills in this book. However, there are times when your particular circumstances would be better served with additional estate planning and possibly consulting an attorney.

Estates over $1,500,000 The wills in this book will pass your estate whether it is $1,000 or $100,000,000. However, if your estate is over $1,500,000, then you might be able to avoid estate taxes by using a trust or some other tax-saving device. The larger your estate, the more you can save on estate taxes by doing more complicated planning. If you have a large estate and are concerned about estate taxes, you should consult an estate planning attorney or a book on estate planning.

Contested Wills If you leave one or more of your children out of your will, it is likely that someone will *contest* your will. If you expect that there may be a fight over your estate or that someone might *contest* your will's validity, then you should consult a lawyer.

Complicated Estate If you are the beneficiary of a trust or have any complications in your legal relationships, such as children from more than one marriage and a second spouse, you may need special provisions in your will.

Conditions If you wish to put some sort of *conditions* or *restrictions* on the property you leave, you should consult a lawyer. For example, if you want to leave money to your brother only if he quits smoking or to a hospital only if they name a wing in your honor, you should consult an attorney to be sure that your conditions are valid.

Blind or Unable to Write A person who is blind or who can sign only with an "X" should consult a lawyer about the proper way to make and execute a will.

ESTATE TAXES

As previously noted, if you have assets worth more than $1,500,000, your estate may be subject to federal estate tax and Texas estate tax. *Estate tax* is a tax imposed on the estate of a decedent. It is a tax imposed on the assets owned by a person at the time of death. The estate tax is calculated on the value of the estate as a whole. The estate taxes must be paid to the Internal Revenue Service and the State of Texas by the executor *before* distributions are made to beneficiaries.

A common misconception about federal estate tax is that life insurance policies, retirement plans, and joint tenancy property are exempt from tax. That is not the case. When a person dies, the value of all of the property owned at the time of death—probate property and nonprobate property—is totaled to determine if his or her estate is large enough to pay estate tax.

NOTE: *It is true that the beneficiaries of a life insurance policy do not have to pay income tax on the amount they receive.*

Federal Estate Tax

The federal estate tax is applied to estates worth over $1,500,000. Estates worth below $1,500,000 are covered by the *unified credit* that exempts the estate from federal estate tax. The *unified credit* determines the amount of property a person can leave to beneficiaries at his or her death or give away during his or her lifetime without paying tax to the Internal Revenue Service. If the value of your estate is more than $1,500,000, a federal estate tax rate of 47% applies.

Example:

Peter has an estate worth $1,700,000. Peter dies in 2005 and his executor applies the unified credit exemption of $1,500,000 to Peter's estate. Only $200,000 of Peter's estate is subject to federal estate tax. However, the estate tax rate is 47%. Therefore, the executor must pay at least $94,000 to the Internal Revenue Service.

Congress passed a law that gradually increases the amount of the *unified credit* to $3,500,000 in 2009. Under that law, in the year 2010, the federal estate tax will be repealed. That is, in 2010 the federal estate tax will no longer be effective. However, that same law provides that in the year 2011 and all subsequent years, the federal estate law becomes effective once again and the unified credit will only be $1,000,000. The following table shows the changes in the unified credit over the next six years.

Estate Tax Rate

Year	Unified Credit Exemption	Over Unified Credit
2005	$1,500,000	47%
2006	$2,000,000	46%
2007	$2,000,000	45%
2008	$2,000,000	45%
2009	$3,500,000	45%
2010	Repealed	N/A
2011	$1,000,000	55%

Federal estate taxes must be paid to the Internal Revenue Service within nine months after your death. Sometimes this can create a hardship for the executor because he or she has to sell assets to raise the money to pay the estate tax. The executor may not be able to get the best price for the assets and might have to sell the assets at a loss in order to pay the estate tax within nine months.

If your estate is worth more than the unified credit amount, there are planning options available to reduce or eliminate the federal estate tax that may be due. Not all such planning options are complicated but the options must be used correctly otherwise they will not accomplish their goal. Often, to effectively use such planning options, documents other than a simple will must be used. Attorneys experienced in estate tax planning can assist you with the preparation of such documents.

Texas Estate Tax Texas does not have its own independent estate tax system. Instead, like many other states, Texas *piggybacks* off of the federal estate tax system. An estate tax will only have to be paid to the State of Texas if your estate is over the unified credit amount. If your estate is over the unified credit amount, the amount of Texas estate tax is calculated using a formula established by the Internal Revenue Service. Like federal estate tax, Texas estate tax must be paid within nine months after your death.

How to Make a Simple Will

There are many things to consider when making your will—*who* are you going to leave *what* to and *when* do you want them to get it? However, while there are several ways you can control how your property will be distributed, you probably have already decided how you want most of it handled and who your beneficiaries will be.

IDENTIFYING PARTIES IN YOUR WILL

When making your will, it is important to clearly identify the people you name as your beneficiaries. In some families, names differ only by middle initial or by Jr. or Sr. Be sure to check everyone's name before making your will. You can also add your relationship to the beneficiary and identify where they live, such as "my cousin, Maxine Martindale of Austin, Texas."

Organizations   The same applies to organizations and charities. For example, more than one group uses the words "cancer society" or "heart association" in their name. Be sure to get the legally correct name of the group that you intend to leave your gift. This can often be done by calling the organization and getting its appropriate legal name. It is also a very good idea to include the address of the organization to reduce the risk of confusion. For example, you can write "American Diabetes Association, Dallas Chapter, 100 Main Street, Dallas, Texas."

Spouse and Children

In most states, you must mention your spouse and children in your will even if you do not leave them any property to show that you are of sound mind and know who are your heirs. If you have a spouse and/or children and plan to leave your property to people other than them, you should consult an attorney to be sure that your will can be enforced.

PERSONAL PROPERTY

Personal property is often referred to in wills or other legal documents. In the case of wills, personal property generally refers to items such as household furnishings, clothes, jewelry, vehicles, and the like. Personal property does not include stocks, bonds, and other investments.

Because people acquire and dispose of personal property so often, it is not advisable to list a lot of small items in your will. Otherwise, when you sell or replace one of them you may have to rewrite your will.

One solution is to describe the type of item you wish to give, rather than the specific item. For example, instead of saying, "I leave my 2004 Ford to my sister," you should say, "I leave any automobile I own at the time of my death to my sister."

Of course, if you do mean to give a specific item, you should describe it. For example, instead of saying "I leave my diamond ring to Joan," you should say, "I leave to Joan the half-carat diamond ring that I inherited from my grandmother," in case you own more than one diamond ring at the time of your death.

Some people write a list of personal property and who will get it, but do not include this list as part of their will. Other people put notes on the actual piece of personal property (such as the back of a picture or the bottom of a piece of furniture) stating who should get that piece of personal property. These methods of designating beneficiaries are not legally enforceable. If you decide to use such a method to give away your personal property, you must be aware of the risk that your executor might not follow your wishes or, if challenged by a beneficiary, will not be approved by the court.

SPECIFIC BEQUESTS

Occasionally a person will want to leave something to a friend or charity and the rest to the family. This can be done with a *specific bequest*, such as "$1,000 to my friend Martha Jones." However, there could be a problem if, at the time of a person's death, there is not anything left after the specific bequests.

Example:

At the time of making his will, Todd had $1,000,000 in assets. He felt generous, so he left $50,000 to a local hospital, $50,000 to a local group that took care of homeless animals, and the rest to his children. Unfortunately, at the time of his death, his estate was worth only $110,000, so after the above specific bequests, the legal fees, and the expenses of probate, there was nothing left for his children.

Another problem with specific bequests is that some of the property might be worth considerably more or less at death than when the will was made.

Example:

Joe wanted his two children to share his estate equally. His will left his son his stocks (worth $500,000 at the time) and his daughter $500,000 in cash. By the time of Joe's death the stock was only worth $100,000, so his son only received $100,000 while his daughter still received the full $500,000.

To accomplish his intended purpose, Joe from the previous example should have left 50% of his estate to each child. It is common to list percentages for each beneficiary so that if the value of your property changes over the years, it will still be divided fairly. If giving certain things to certain people is an important part of your estate plan, you can do it, but remember to change your will if your assets change.

Joint Beneficiaries

Be careful about leaving one item of personal property to more than one person. For example, if you leave something to your son *and* his wife, what happens if they divorce? Even if you leave something to two of your own children, what if they cannot agree about who will have possession of it? Whenever possible, leave property to only one person.

REMAINDER CLAUSE

One of the most important clauses in a will is the *remainder clause* (sometimes called the *residue clause*). This is the clause that says something like "all the rest of my property I leave to…". This clause ensures that the will disposes of all property owned at the time of death that is not given away by a specific bequest so that nothing is forgotten.

In a simple will, the best way to distribute property is to put it all in the remainder clause. In the first example in the previous section about Todd, the problem would have been avoided if the will had read as follows: "The rest, residue, and remainder of my estate I leave 50% to ABC Hospital, 5% to XYZ Animal Welfare League, and 90% to be divided equally among my children…."

ALTERNATE BENEFICIARIES

You should always provide for an *alternate beneficiary,* or a person who will inherit your estate in case the person you name dies before you and you do not have a chance to make out a new will.

Survivor or Descendants

Suppose your will leaves your property to your sister and brother but your brother predeceases you. Should his share go to your sister or your brother's children or grandchildren? If you are giving property to two or more people and you want it all to go to the other if one of them dies, then you must specify "or the survivor of them." For example, "to my sister, Judith, and my brother, Tom, in equal shares or all to the survivor of them."

If, on the other hand, you want the property to go to the children of the deceased person, you should state in your will, "to their lineal descendants." For example, "to my sister, Judith, and my brother, Tom, in equal shares. If either of Judith or Tom does not survive me, his or her share will go to his or her lineal descendants." This includes his or her children and grandchildren.

Family or Person

If you decide you want property to go to your brother's children and grandchildren, you must also decide if an equal share should go to each family or to each person. For example, if your brother leaves three grandchildren and one is an only child of his daughter and the others are the children of his son, should all grandchildren get equal shares or should they split their parent's share?

When you want each family to get an equal share it is called *per stirpes*. When you want each person to get an equal share it is called *per capita*.

Example:

Alice leaves her property to her two daughters, Mary and Pat, in equal shares, or to their lineal descendants per stirpes. Both daughters die before Alice. Mary leaves one child; Pat leaves two children. In this case, Mary's child gets half of the estate and Pat's children split the other half of the estate. If Alice had specified per capita instead of per stirpes, then each child would have gotten one-third of the estate.

Per Stirpes Distribution

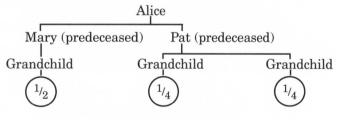

Per Capita Distribution

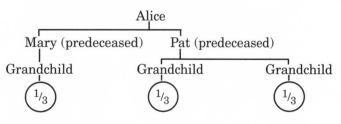

Most of the wills in this book use per stirpes because that is the most common way property is left. If you wish to leave your property per capita, then you can rewrite the will with using per capita instead of per stirpes.

There are fourteen different will forms in this book that should cover most situations, but you may want to divide your property slightly differently from what is stated in these forms. If so, you can retype the forms according to your wishes, specifying whether the property should go to the survivor or the lineal descendants. If you have any questions, you should seek the advice of an attorney.

SURVIVORSHIP

Many people put a clause in their will stating that anyone receiving property under the will must survive for a certain period of time—thirty, forty-five, or sixty days—after the death of the person who made the will. This provision is so that if the two people die in the same accident, there will not be two probates, and the property will not go to the other party's heirs.

Example:

Fred and Wilma were married and each had children by previous marriages. In their wills, Fred and Wilma left all their property to each other. If the spouse was not alive, all of the person's property went to his or her own children. They did not have survivorship clauses in their wills, and they were in an airplane crash and died. Fred's children hired several expert witnesses and a law firm to prove that at the time of the crash, Fred lived for a few minutes longer than Wilma. So, when Wilma died first, all of her property went to Fred. When he died a few minutes later, all of Fred *and* Wilma's property went to his children. Wilma's children got nothing.

GUARDIANS FOR CHILDREN

If you have minor children, you should name a guardian for them. There are two types of guardians—a guardian over the *person* and a guardian over the *property*. The guardian over the person decides where the children will live and makes the other parental decisions for them. A guardian over the property is in charge of the minor's property and inheritance. In most cases, one person is appointed guardian over both the person and property. But some people prefer the children to live with one person, but to have the money held by another person.

Example:

Sandra was a widow with a young daughter. She knew that if anything happened to her, her sister would be the best person to raise her daughter. But her sister was never good with money. So when Sandra wrote her will, she named her sister as guardian over the person of her daughter, and she named her father as guardian over the property of her daughter.

When naming a guardian, it is always advisable to name an *alternate guardian,* or a person to serve as guardian in case your first choice is unable to serve for any reason.

Many times parents name their brother or sister or a trusted friend to be the guardian of their children. Often, if the guardian is married, a person names his or her brother, sister, etc., guardian *and* that person's spouse to be the guardians. This may cause problems if the guardian gets a divorce or dies and his or her spouse is still alive. The children may end up being raised by a person who was not intended to be the guardian. If you have this situation, you should consider naming only one person to be guardian.

Example:

Henry is a widower and has three minor children. He wants his brother, Sam, to be guardian of his children and names his sister, Heather, as alternate guardian. Sam is married to Sally. Henry's will names Sam and Sally as guardians. After Henry's death, Sam and Sally are guardians. Sam dies while the children are minors and Sally gets to keep the children. Henry's sister Heather does not get them at Sam's death like Henry wanted.

You may also want your children to be raised in a home with a married couple. You can include a provision that states if the guardians you name get divorced, the children will be raised by the alternate guardians you name in your will.

Custodial Accounts for Minors

Under Texas law, a child cannot legally inherit property until the age of 18. If a parent dies and the child is under age 18, the courts require that special accounts be established for any cash or investments given to the child. A custodian is named to manage the special accounts. The custodian is required to use the property only for the child and often has to get court permission to spend money in the account. The custodian can often be the same person who is named as the guardian of the child.

In the example on page 35, Sandra's father, who she named as guardian of the children's property, would be the custodian named to control the special accounts. If Sandra had not designated her father to be guardian of the children's property, Sandra's sister may have been named as the custodian of the special accounts.

Disinheriting Children

Under Texas law, you can decide to leave nothing to your children *provided your children are not minors*. (If your children are minors, Texas law makes certain that they will receive a certain amount of your estate so that the minor children will have a means of support.) If your children are adults, you can disinherit them. Unlike popular belief, you do not have to leave a child (or any other person) $1.00 in order to disinherit them. However, if you choose to disinherit an adult child, you should include a specific statement in your will that says you intend to disinherit them. For example, you can include "I have specifically made no provision for my child, Ben, because it is my intention that he receive nothing from my estate." Including a statement such as this helps to avoid a contest to your will by Ben claiming that you forgot to include a gift to him.

CHILDREN'S TRUST

When a parent dies leaving a minor child, and the child's property is held by a guardian, in Texas the guardianship ends when the child reaches the age of 18. At that point, all of the property is turned over to the child. Most parents do not feel their children are competent at the age of 18 to handle large sums of money and prefer that it be held until the child is 21, 25, 30, or even older.

If you wish to set up a system of determining when your children should receive various amounts of your estate, or if you want the property held to a higher age than 35, you should consult a lawyer to draft a trust. However, if you want a simple provision that the funds be held until the children reach a higher age than 18, and you trust someone to make decisions about paying for education or other expenses for your child or children, you can put that provision in your will as a *children's trust*.

The children's trust trustee can be the same person as the guardian or a different person. It is advisable to name an alternate trustee in case your first choice is unable to handle the trust.

NOTE: *The forms included in this book include provisions dealing with the designation of a guardian for your minor children, a guardian of your minor children's property, and children's trusts. You can adapt the forms to include some of the special provisions discussed in the preceding sections. In addition, Chapter 9 includes a discussion of additional forms regarding the custody and medical care of your minor children during your lifetime and after you have passed away.*

TRUSTS FOR PARENTS

Today it is not uncommon for a parent to live longer than his or her adult child. With the high cost of medical care, assisted living, and nursing homes, an adult child may wish to set aside some part of his or her estate in trust for the benefit of his or her parents.

If the parent is receiving Medicaid or some other form of government assistance *or* lives in a residential facility that requires all of a resident's assets be turned over to the facility for the resident's care, the child should keep property in a trust for the benefit of his or her parent. This type of planning is very complex and many state and federal rules must be followed. If you are considering such a provision for your will, consult an attorney who is familiar with Medicaid planning and trusts for the elderly.

EXECUTOR

An *executor* is the person who will be in charge of your probate. He or she will gather your assets, handle the sale of them if necessary, prepare an inventory, hire an attorney, and distribute the property. If this is a person you trust, then you can state in your will that no bond will be required to be posted by him or her. Otherwise, the court will require that a *surety bond* be paid for by your estate to guaranty that the person is honest. You can appoint a bank to handle your estate, but bank fees are usually very high.

It is best to appoint a resident of Texas because it is easier for the executor to perform his or her duties if the person resides in the area. Also, a bond might be required of a nonresident, even if your will waives the requirement.

Some people like to name two people to handle their estate to avoid jealousy or to have them check on each other's honesty. However, this makes double the work in getting the papers signed and creates problems if they cannot agree on something.

Alternate Executor   When naming an executor, it is always advisable to name an *alternate executor* or a person to serve as executor in case your first choice is unable to serve for any reason. This is especially important if you are naming a person who is older than you. In the event that person dies before you do, the alternate executor would be able to serve and you do not have to do a new will when your first choice dies.

WITNESSES

A will must be witnessed by two people to be valid in Texas. In all states except Vermont, only two witnesses are required. Unless you own property in Vermont, you do not need more than two witnesses. The witness must be at least 14 years old, however, it is best to have witnesses who are over the age of 18.

In Texas it is legal for a beneficiary of a will to be a witness to the will, but not recommended. It can cause problems, especially if there is anyone who may contest your will, to have a beneficiary or family member be a witness to your will.

SELF-PROVING AFFIDAVIT

As previously mentioned, a will only needs two witnesses to be legal, but if it includes a *self-proving affidavit* and is notarized, then the will can be admitted to probate quickly. If the will is *not* self-proved, then one of the witnesses must testify in court and sign a sworn statement that the will is genuine.

A self-proved will means that an *affidavit* is attached to the will. The affidavit states that the person making the will is over the age of 18, is of sound mind, and has stated that the will accurately reflects his or her intentions. The affidavit also states that the witnesses are over the age of 14, that the person acknowledged that it was his or her will, and that the witnesses signed the will in the presence and at the request of the person. The person making the will and the witnesses sign the affidavit under oath in front of a notary public.

The purpose of a self-proved will is to avoid the complications of finding a witness after your death and bringing that witness to court to testify that your will was validly executed under Texas law. A **SELF-PROVING AFFIDAVIT** is included as form 19 in Appendix D.

In an emergency situation (for example, if you are bedridden and there is no notary available), you can execute your will without the self-proving affidavit. As long as it has two witnesses, it will be valid.

The only drawback is that at least one of the witnesses will later have to go to court, testify, and sign an oath.

DISINHERITING SOMEONE

If you intend to disinherit someone, you should not make your own will (without an attorney), because it may result in your will being challenged in court. However, you may make your own will if you wish to leave one child less of your estate than another because you already made a gift to that child or if that child needs the money less than the other. If you do give more to one child than to another, then you should state your reasons to prove that you thought about your plan. Otherwise the one who receives less might argue that you did not realize what you were doing and were not competent to make a will.

FUNERAL ARRANGEMENTS

There is no harm in stating your funeral preferences in your will, but in most states, including Texas, directions for a funeral are not legally enforceable. Often a will is not found until after the funeral. Therefore it is better to tell your family about your wishes or to make prior arrangements yourself.

HANDWRITTEN WILLS

In Texas, a person can handwrite a will without any witnesses, and it will be held valid. A handwritten will is called a *holographic will*. It must be entirely in your own handwriting and clearly express your intention to make it your will. Since there is a greater chance an unwitnessed handwritten will will be held invalid, you should only use one in an emergency, such as if you are ill and unable to locate any witnesses.

FORMS

There are more than twenty different forms included in this book for easy use. You can either cut them out, photocopy them, or retype them on plain paper. Each is also available on the accompanying CD-ROM for even easier and quicker use.

The forms in this book are printed on both sides of the page. If you photocopy them on separate pages or print your will on more than one piece of paper, you should staple the pages together, initial each page, and have both witnesses initial each page. Each page should state at the bottom, "page 1 of 3," "page 2 of 3," etc.

CORRECTIONS

Your will should have no white-outs or erasures. If for some reason it is impossible to make a will without corrections, each correction should be initialed by you and both witnesses.

Checklist for Planning Your Will

☐ Do you have the correct legal names of all of the people you are naming in your will—executors, guardians, beneficiaries and organizations?

☐ Have you prepared a list of your property including names and numbers of bank accounts, investment accounts, retirement accounts, life insurance policies, annuities, and other property? Can this information easily be located by your family after your death?

☐ Have you made funeral arrangements and made your family and friends aware of these plans?

☐ Have you named an *executor* who you trust to handle your assets after you die and make certain that your wishes are carried out?

continued

☐ Do you want your executor to be able to administer your estate without unnecessary court supervision and expense? If so, you should include language designating your executor as an *independent executor*.

☐ Do you trust that the executor will not steal your property? If not, you should include language that requires your executor to post *bond* with the court.

☐ Have you named an *alternate* person to serve as executor if your first choice cannot serve?

☐ Have you named a *guardian* of your minor children you trust to raise your minor children and give them the type of home and upbringing that you would give them?

☐ Have you named an *alternate* person to serve as guardian if your first choice cannot serve?

☐ Who do you trust to take care of the money and property that you give to your minor children? Is this person the same person who will raise your children? If not, this person should be named as guardian of the *estate* (property) of the minor children.

☐ Have you named an *alternate* person to serve as guardian of the estate if your first choice cannot serve?

☐ Do you want the money left for your minor children to be given to them at age 18? If not, at what ages should the children receive the money?

☐ If you want your money to be given to your children after the age of 18, who will be in charge of the *Children's Trust*? This person should be named as *trustee* of the Children's Trust.

☐ Have you named an *alternate* person to serve as trustee if your first choice cannot serve?

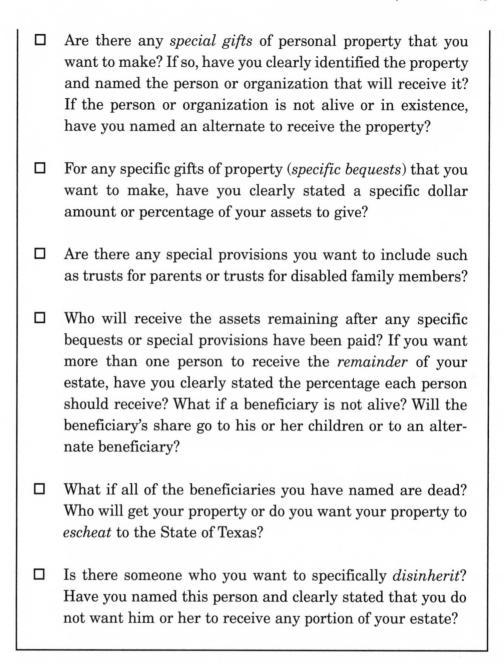

☐ Are there any *special gifts* of personal property that you want to make? If so, have you clearly identified the property and named the person or organization that will receive it? If the person or organization is not alive or in existence, have you named an alternate to receive the property?

☐ For any specific gifts of property (*specific bequests*) that you want to make, have you clearly stated a specific dollar amount or percentage of your assets to give?

☐ Are there any special provisions you want to include such as trusts for parents or trusts for disabled family members?

☐ Who will receive the assets remaining after any specific bequests or special provisions have been paid? If you want more than one person to receive the *remainder* of your estate, have you clearly stated the percentage each person should receive? What if a beneficiary is not alive? Will the beneficiary's share go to his or her children or to an alternate beneficiary?

☐ What if all of the beneficiaries you have named are dead? Who will get your property or do you want your property to *escheat* to the State of Texas?

☐ Is there someone who you want to specifically *disinherit*? Have you named this person and clearly stated that you do not want him or her to receive any portion of your estate?

How to Execute Your Will

Signing a will is a serious legal event, and it must be done properly or the will can be declared invalid. Preferably, it should be done in a private room without distraction. All parties must watch each other sign, and no one should leave the area until all have signed.

Example:
Ebenezer was bedridden in a small room. His will was brought in to him to sign, but the witnesses could not actually see his hand signing because a dresser was in the way. His will was ignored by the court and his property went to two people who were not in his will.

Procedure   To be sure your will is valid, follow these rules.

✪   Say to your witnesses, "This is my will. I have read it, I understand it, and this is how I want it to read. I want you two (or three) people to be my witnesses." Contrary to popular belief, you do not have to read the will to the witnesses or let them read it.

✪   Date your will and sign your name at the end in ink exactly as it is printed in the will.

✪   Initial each page as both witnesses watch.

✪   Watch with the other witnesses as each party signs at the end in ink.

Self-Proving Affidavit

As explained in the last chapter, it is important to attach a self-proving affidavit to your will. You will need to have a notary public present to watch everyone sign. If it is impossible to have a notary present, your will is still valid, but the probate process might be delayed and may be more complicated.

After your witnesses have signed as attesting witnesses under your name, you all should sign the self-proving page and the notary should notarize it. The notary should not be one of your witnesses.

It is a good idea to make at least one *copy* of your will, but do not personally sign any copies or have them notarized. The reason for this is if you cancel or destroy your will, someone may produce a signed copy of your old will and have it probated. This would be contrary to your intentions. Also, if you lose or accidentally destroy a notarized copy of your will, a court may assume you intended to revoke the original will.

Example:

Michael typed out a copy of his will and made two photocopies. He had the original and both copies signed and notarized. He then gave the original to his sister, who was his executor, and kept the two copies. Upon his death, the two copies could not be found. Because these copies were in his possession, it was assumed that he destroyed them. A court ruled that by destroying them, he must have intended to revoke the original will, and his property went to people not listed in his will.

STORING YOUR WILL

Your will should be kept in a place safe from fire and easily accessible to your heirs. Your executor should know where it is. It can be kept in a home safe or a firebox. Also, in Texas, a will can be removed from a safe-deposit box in a bank without many complications, so you can keep it there.

If you are close to your children and can trust them, then you can allow one of them to keep the will in his or her safe-deposit box. However, if you later decide to limit that child's share of your estate or omit the child from your will, there could be a problem.

Example:

Diane wrote her will giving her property to her two children equally and gave the will to her older child, Bill, to hold. Years later, Bill moved away, and her younger child, Mary, took care of her every day. Diane made a new will giving most of her property to Mary. Upon Diane's death, Bill came to town and found the new will in Diane's house. He destroyed it and probated the old will, which gave him half the property.

chapter 6

After You Sign Your Will

Once you execute your will, you are essentially finished. However, it is a document that needs to change as your circumstances change, and you need to understand the proper way to change it or revoke it all together.

REVIEWING YOUR WILL

After you have signed your will, you should not put it in a drawer or a safe-deposit box and forget about it. At least once a year, review your will to determine whether the will still accurately reflects your intentions. In addition to reviewing the checklist at the end of Chapter 5, you should also consider the following questions.

Have you been divorced? If so, rewrite your will and remove all references to your former spouse. If you intend to include your former spouse as a beneficiary, executor, or trustee, you should still write a new will after the divorce is finalized. You may also wish to include a specific sentence that states it is your intention that your former spouse be included in the will.

Have you been married? If so, you should rewrite your will to include your spouse as a beneficiary or, if you have signed a prenuptial agreement, you should include a provision that clearly states a prenuptial agreement has been signed and include the date on which it was signed.

Have you had children? If so, you may wish to rewrite your will to include the new child. However, if your original will includes language that automatically includes any children born after the date of that will, there may be no need to rewrite your will.

Have there been any changes in the custody of your children that affect your will? Many times, a noncustodial parent does not include a provision in his or her will designating a guardian for minor children. If the custodial parent dies and the noncustodial parent gets custody, that parent must make sure a guardianship designation is included in his or her will.

Have there been any deaths that affect the executor, guardian, or trustee designations in your will? If a person you have named as executor, guardian, or trustee has died and your will does not name an alternate, you should rewrite your will to name a new executor, guardian, or trustee. If your will names an alternate, you may also wish to rewrite your will to name an alternate to your alternate.

Has a beneficiary died? If so, does your will provide an alternate beneficiary? If your will does not provide an alternate beneficiary, your will should be rewritten to make certain that the property will be given to individuals you choose. Also, if a beneficiary has died, that may change your mind as to the division of your property among the remaining beneficiaries.

Has a beneficiary, executor, guardian, or trustee remarried? If so, are you concerned that the new spouse might unduly influence or interfere with the rights and duties of a beneficiary, executor, guardian, or trustee?

Has an organization named as a beneficiary changed its purposes or is no longer in existence? If an organization named in your will is no longer in existence and no alternate beneficiary is named, you may need to change your will to either delete the gift or name an alternate organization. If the organization has changed its purposes or you do not agree with the manner in which it is conducting its business, you may need to change your will to delete the gift.

Do you need to make additional provisions for disabled or minor beneficiaries? Is there a friend or family member who has become disabled and is in need of financial assistance? Are there any minor children of family or friends to whom you want to leave a financial gift? Again, a change to your will may be necessary to accommodate this new circumstance.

Has the size of your estate increased or decreased? If your estate has grown in value, do you need to include provisions to reduce or eliminate estate taxes? If your estate has grown in value, do you want to include additional beneficiaries? If your estate has decreased in value, will this affect any gifts made in your will? Depending on the size of your estate, changes may be necessary to maximize what you can leave tax free.

Have you changed your mind about beneficiaries, executors, guardians, or trustees? If you have had second thoughts about gifts you made in your will or the people you have named as executor, guardian, or trustee, you should change your will.

CHANGING YOUR WILL

Even if you do not change your mind about provisions in your will, certain events will automatically override provisions of your will.

Marriage If you get married after you have made your will and you do not rewrite it after the wedding, your spouse is entitled to a share of your estate as if you had no will. The only exceptions to this rule are if you have a prenuptial agreement or you made a provision for your spouse in the will prior to your marriage. However, you must remember that any property acquired after your marriage (including income earned by the investments you had prior to your marriage) will be community property and your spouse is entitled to one-half of the community property.

Divorce   If you get divorced after making your will and do not rewrite it after the divorce is finalized, all provisions in the will for your spouse are void including the nomination of your spouse as executor of the estate or as trustee of any property you leave in trust for your children.

Example:

Mark and Barb execute wills during their marriage leaving two-thirds of their separate and community property to each other and one-third in trust for their children. Mark and Barb are named executors of each other's wills and trustees of the children's trust. After their divorce, all provisions leaving property to each other and the nominations as executor and trustee are void.

If you intend to allow your former spouse to act as executor of your estate or trustee of the children's trust, you must make a new will or make a *codicil* (an amendment to a will) after the date on which the divorce is final. The new will or codicil should make clear that it is your intention that your former spouse serve as executor or trustee. In addition, if you want to give property to your former spouse, you can do so in the new will or codicil.

Children   If you have a child after making your will and do not rewrite your will, the child may receive a share of your estate as if there were no will.

Example:

Dave makes a will leaving half of his estate to his sister and the other half to be shared by his three children, John, Alice, and Bob, whom he names in the will. He later has another child and does not revise his will. Upon his death, his sister receives half of the estate and the other half of the estate is divided equally among his four children.

It is best to rewrite your will at the birth of a child. However, another solution is to include a clause that makes clear that your will automatically includes all of your children. Such a provision may read as follows:

I intend to include all of my children named in this will as well as any children born after the date of this will.

Codicil vs. a New Will

You can change your will by revoking your existing will and signing a new will or by making a *codicil* to your will. A codicil is an amendment to your will. A codicil can delete a provision in your will, add a provision to your will, or change an existing a provision in your will. A codicil must be executed with the same formalities as a will. Therefore, a codicil must be signed by you and by two witnesses. For the codicil to be made self-proving, a self-proving affidavit must be attached to the codicil. Thus, a notary public must notarize the codicil.

Because a codicil must be executed with the same formalities as a will, it is often desirable to sign a new will. Also, it is not desirable to have more than one codicil to a will. Therefore, if you have already executed a codicil and want to make an additional change to your will, instead of making a second codicil, you should sign a new will. If you do want to make a small change, a **CODICIL** form is included in Appendix D. (see form 20, p.141.)

If you decide to remove a gift to a beneficiary, you might want to sign a new will because a new will has no references to the beneficiary you are disinheriting. If a person is named as beneficiary and then a codicil is made to delete their gift, the disgruntled beneficiary may choose to contest the will and codicil.

REVOKING YOUR WILL

The usual way to *revoke* a will is to execute a new one that states that it revokes all previously made wills. To revoke a will without making a new one, you can tear, burn, cancel, deface, obliterate, or destroy it, as long as you do this with the intention of revoking the will. If it is destroyed accidentally, the will is not legally revoked.

Example:
Ralph tells his son, Clyde, to go to the basement safe to tear up his (Ralph's) will. However, if Clyde does not tear it up in Ralph's presence, it is probably not effectively revoked.

Revival   If you change your will by drafting a new one, and later decide you do not like the changes, you cannot destroy the new one and revive the old one. Once you execute a new will revoking an old will, you cannot revive the old will unless you execute a new document stating that you intend to revive the old will. In other words, it is easier to execute a new will.

chapter 7

Living Wills and Health Care Agents

Texas has two documents that can be signed by a person to leave instructions regarding his or her health care in the event a person cannot make such decisions and communicate them to health care providers. These documents are a Living Will and a Health Care Power of Attorney.

LIVING WILLS

A *living will* is a document in which a person declares that he or she does not want artificial life support systems used if he or she becomes terminally ill. Modern science can often keep a body alive even if the brain is permanently dead or the person is in constant pain. All states have legalized living wills either by statute or by court decision. In Texas, this document is called a *directive*. It has nothing to do with the usual type of will that distributes property.

A *directive* must be signed in front of two witnesses who should not be blood relatives or a spouse. If the person is physically unable to sign, he or she may read the *directive* out loud and direct one of the witnesses to sign it for him or her. A *directive* can be in the form included in the Texas statutes or it can be rewritten. But to be sure it will be valid, it is best to use the statutory form. (see form 21, p.145.)

MEDICAL POWER OF ATTORNEY

There may be a time when a person is unable to make decisions regarding his or her routine medical care. This may occur when a person has been in an automobile accident, is unconscious, and is unable to talk with doctors about tests, x-rays, or even surgery that may be needed. In this situation, an individual designated by the patient as a *health care agent* can make such decisions until the patient regains the ability to make decisions regarding routine medical care. The basic purpose of this form is to designate a person who can provide doctors and medical professionals with *informed consent* to medical procedures on behalf of a patient.

In Texas, a **MEDICAL POWER OF ATTORNEY AND DESIGNATION OF HEALTH CARE AGENT** can be signed by a person in advance of such situations. Then, in the event the need arises, the health care agent can present the document to the doctors and make health care decisions. This form must be signed in front of two witnesses who should not be blood relatives, a spouse, or a medical professional. The statutory **MEDICAL POWER OF ATTORNEY AND DESIGNATION OF HEALTH CARE AGENT** form is included in Appendix D as form 22, p.147.

It is often recommended that a copy of the **MEDICAL POWER OF ATTORNEY AND DESIGNATION OF HEALTH CARE AGENT** be given to the person who is named as the health care agent as well as your primary care physician to be made part of your medical records. In the event a different agent is later named, the new medical power of attorney should be given to the primary care physician and it should be made clear that the earlier document is of no effect and should be destroyed.

chapter 8

How to Designate a Guardian for Yourself

As our population lives longer, it has become increasingly common for a guardianship to be established for an older individual. This process requires the involvement of the court. The court may appoint a family member, friend, or an unrelated party to serve as a person's guardian. The person for whom the guardianship is being obtained (often called the *ward*) has no input into who will serve as his or her guardian. Among family members, it may be a race to the courthouse to see who will be appointed as guardian. The court would have to find compelling reasons not to appoint a particular family member as guardian. Mere allegations that the family member and the ward do not get along will not keep that family member from being appointed.

Texas law permits a person to designate someone to serve as his or her guardian in the event the person becomes incapacitated and must have a guardian. The statutory form is included in Appendix D as form 23, p.153.

There are two important distinctions on this form. First, a person can designate a *guardian of my person*. Such a guardian will be responsible for making decisions regarding health care, basic living conditions, and basic personal decisions for a person. The second designation is a *guardian of my estate*. This guardian will be responsible for handling financial matters such as bank accounts, investments, bills, health insurance benefits, and the like. Many times the same person will serve as guardian of the person and estate. However, one person may be better suited to make health care decisions and another person may be better suited to make financial decisions.

Example:

Suzanne is 70 years old and wants to designate a guardian in the event she becomes incapacitated. She appoints Elizabeth, who is a nurse, to be guardian of her person and appoints Mike, who is an accountant, to be guardian of her estate.

This form also permits a person to specifically disqualify someone from serving as a guardian. This situation may arise if a person is estranged from a parent, child, or some other family member and wants to make clear that such person should not be appointed to serve as guardian.

How to Designate a Guardian and Health Care Agent for Your Children

chapter 9

Texas law contains two important documents that a person can sign relating to the welfare of his or her children. The first ensures the guardianship of minor children, and the second assures medical treatment for children during a parent's absence.

The first document is the **DECLARATION OF APPOINTMENT OF GUARDIAN FOR MY CHILDREN IN THE EVENT OF MY DEATH OR INCAPACITY**. This statutory form is included in Appendix D as form 24.

If a parent dies with a will and has designated a guardian for his or her minor children, the guardian provisions in the will control. However, if a parent dies without a will (or dies with a will that does not contain a guardianship designation) but has signed a **DECLARATION OF APPOINTMENT OF GUARDIAN**, the court will give preference to such designation unless the court finds that it is not in the best interests of the children to be raised by the person designated.

If a parent becomes incapacitated, whether permanently or temporarily, it is very important that his or her wishes be known as to who will raise the minor children during the period of incapacity. Many times family members will argue about who will take care of the children and may have to go to court to have the differences settled. A **DECLARATION OF APPOINTMENT OF GUARDIAN** would avoid this family squabbling.

Example:

Jane is a single parent, and is in a car accident and has suffered head injuries. She will require several months of hospitalization and rehabilitation. Her ex-husband lives in another state and is unable to take care of the children. Jane had signed a **DECLARATION OF APPOINTMENT OF GUARDIAN** naming her sister as guardian. Her sister would have all the legal rights of a guardian of the children until Jane recovers.

The second document is the **AUTHORIZATION TO CONSENT TO MEDICAL TREATMENT**. If a parent is traveling and leaving a child in the temporary care and custody of friends or relatives, the parent can complete the **AUTHORIZATION TO CONSENT TO MEDICAL TREATMENT**. This document authorizes the temporary custodian to consent to medical and dental treatment for the child during the specific period of the parent's absence.

The **AUTHORIZATION TO CONSENT TO MEDICAL TREATMENT** can also be given to a temporary custodian for a child for general periods of time such as weekend visitations, periods of day care, or the like. Such authorization can be given to grandparents, relatives, and day care providers who will have custody of the child on a frequent basis.

The statutory form used for the **AUTHORIZATION TO CONSENT TO MEDICAL TREATMENT** is included in Appendix D as forms 25 and 26. Form 25 is used for *general* periods of time. Form 26 is used for a *specific* period of time. Both forms can be revised as necessary for use by one parent or both parents.

chapter 10

How to Make Anatomical Gifts

Texas residents are allowed to donate their bodies or organs for research or transplantation. Consent may be given by a relative of a deceased person, but because relatives are often in shock or too upset to make such a decision, it is better to have one's intent made clear before death. Consent can be given through a statement in a will or through another signed document such as a **UNIFORM DONOR CARD**. (see form 27, p.161.) Texas residents may also make such a statement on the back of their driver's licenses. The gift may include all or only part of one's body. It may be made to a specific person, such as a physician or an ill relative.

The document making the donation must be signed before two witnesses, who must also sign in each other's presence. If the donor cannot sign, then the document may be signed for him or her at his or her direction in the presence of the witnesses. The donor may even designate in the document which physician will carry out the procedure.

If the document or will has been delivered to a specific donee, it may be amended or revoked by the donor through:

- ✪ the execution and delivery of a signed statement to the donee;

- ✪ an oral statement to two witnesses who tell the donee;

- ✪   an oral statement during a terminal illness made to an attending physician who tells the donee; or,

- ✪   a signed document found with the donor or in his or her effects.

If a document of donation has not been delivered to a donee, it may be revoked by any of the above methods or by destruction, cancellation, or mutilation of the document. It may also be revoked in the same method a will is revoked as described on page 53.

Glossary

A

administrator (*administratrix* if female)**.** A person appointed by the court to oversee distribution of the property of someone who died either without a will, or if the person designated in the will is unable to serve.

alternate beneficiary. A person who is entitled to receive property from a person who died, only if the first beneficiary named is not alive or is not entitled to receive the property.

annual exclusion. The amount of property a person can give to another person per year that is not counted against the lifetime unified credit.

attested will. A will that includes an attestation clause and has been signed in front of witnesses and notary public.

B

beneficiary. A person who is entitled to receive property from a person who died (regardless of whether there is a will).

bequest. Personal property (including cash, stocks, etc.) left to someone in a will.

C

children's trust. A trust set up to hold property given to children. Usually it provides that the children will not receive their property until they reach a higher age than the age of majority.

codicil. An amendment to a will.

community property. Property acquired during marriage that was not a gift to or inheritance of one spouse or is specifically kept separate. This includes wages, income on investments, and income from business.

D

decedent. A person who has died.

declaration of guardian in advance of later incapacity or need of guardian. A document by which a person designates one or more persons to act as his or her guardian in the event the person becomes incapacitated.

dependent estate administration. Executor's actions and records are audited or approved by the probate court. Executor is required to obtain court's prior approval to pay debts, collects assets, pay taxes, or distribute assets to beneficiaries.

descendent. A child, grandchild, great-grandchild, etc.

devise. Real property left to someone in a will. A person who is entitled to a devise is called a *devisee*.

E

elective share. In noncommunity property states, the portion of the estate that may be taken by a surviving spouse, regardless of what the will says.

executor (*executrix* if female). A person appointed in a will to oversee distribution of the property of someone who died with a will.

estate tax. Type of death tax based on the decedent's right to transfer property; not a tax on the property itself.

exempt property. Property that is exempt from distribution as a normal part of the estate.

F

family allowance. An amount deemed reasonable by the court that is paid to the surviving spouse and children of the decedent to defray living expenses during the year following death.

federal estate tax. Federal tax assessed against the assets of a person who has died if the value of the taxable assets exceeds the unified credit.

forced share. *See elective share.*

G

guardian of incompetent. Person or corporation appointed by a court to handle the affairs or property of another who is unable to do so because of incapacity.

guardian of minor child. Person or persons named to have custody of and raise minor children.

H

handwritten will. (Also known as a holographic will.) All material provisions are entirely in the handwriting of the maker and the will is signed by the maker.

heir. A person who will inherit from a decedent who died without a will.

holographic will. A will in which all of the material provisions are entirely in the handwriting of the maker. Holographic wills are legal in Texas.

homestead. A person's principal place of residence as designated with the county recorder.

I

incapacitated/incompetent. One who is unable to manage his or her own affairs either temporarily or permanently.

independent estate administration. Executor's actions and records are not audited or approved by the probate court. Executor is not required to obtain court's prior approval to pay debts, collects assets, pay taxes, or distribute assets to beneficiaries.

inheritance tax. Tax imposed on property received by beneficiaries from the estate of a decedent.

intestate. Without making a will. One who dies without a will is said to have *died intestate*.

intestate share. In noncommunity property states, the portion of the estate a spouse is entitled to receive if there is no will.

J

joint tenancy. A type of property ownership by two or more persons, in which if one owner dies, that owner's interest goes to the other joint tenants (not to the deceased owner's heirs as in tenancy in common).

joint tenancy with right of survivorship (JTWROS). Form of ownership in which property is equally shared by all owners and is automatically transferred to the surviving owners when one of them dies.

L

legacy. Real property left to someone in a will. A person who is entitled to a legacy is called a *legatee*.

living (or inter vivos) trust. A revocable trust separate from a will that may be funded or unfunded during the settlor's lifetime. It is commonly used to avoid probate and provide a means for the management of assets during incompetency or incapacity.

living will. A document expressing the writer's desires regarding how medical care is to be handled in the event the writer is not able to express his or her wishes concerning the use of life-prolonging medical procedures.

M

medical power of attorney. A document that designates one or more persons to make routine health care decisions in the event a person is unable to give informed consent and make such decisions him- or herself.

P

payable on death account (POD). An account that is automatically paid to a beneficiary named by the owner of the account upon the death of the account owner. The beneficiary has no rights to the account during his or her lifetime.

per capita. Distribution of property with equal shares going to each person.

per stirpes. Distribution of property with equal shares going to each family line.

personal property. Property that is movable, not land or things attached to land.

personal property memorandum. A document separate from the will that designates distribution of personal effects. This document is not legally effective but evidences a person's intent regarding distribution of personal effects.

personal representative. A person appointed by the court, or will, to oversee distribution of the property of the person who died. This is a more modern term than "administrator," "executor," etc., and applies regardless of whether there is a will.

power of attorney. Legal document whereby one person authorizes another to make medical and financial decisions should illness or incapacitation occur.

probate. Legal process of establishing the validity of a deceased person's last will and testament; commonly refers to the process and laws for settling an estate.

R

real property. Property that's immovable, such as land, buildings, and whatever else is attached to or growing on land.

residue. The property that is left over in an estate after all specific bequests and devises.

S

self-proving affidavit. A form added to a will in which the will maker and witnesses state under oath in front of a notary public that they have signed and witnessed the will.

separate property. Property owned by a spouse prior to marriage or acquired by the spouse during marriage by gift, inheritance, or as a result of a personal injury settlement.

specific bequest/specific devise. A gift in a will of a specific item of property or a specific amount of cash.

statutory will. A will that has been prepared according to the requirements of a statute.

T

tenancy by entirety. Form of spousal ownership in which property is equally shared and automatically transferred to the surviving spouse. While both spouses are living, ownership of the property can be altered only by divorce or mutual agreement.

tenancy in common. Ownership of property by two or more people, in which each owner's share descends to that owner's heirs (not to the other owners as in joint tenancy).

testamentary trust. Trust established in a person's will.

testate. With a will. One who dies with a will is said to have *died testate*.

testator (*testatrix* if female)**.** A person who makes his or her will.

Totten trust. Revocable trust created by the owner of a bank account (checking, savings, or other) for the future benefit of another.

trust. Real or personal property held by one party (the trustee) for the benefit of another (the beneficiary).

trustee. Person who holds and/or manages money or property for the benefit of another.

U

unified credit. The federal credit against estate taxes that is allowed to each person or estate.

W

will. Legal document that declares how a person wishes property to be distributed to heirs or beneficiaries after death. It can only be enforced through a probate court.

Selected Provisions of Texas Probate Code

The following are some selected provisions of the Texas Probate Code regarding distribution if you do not have a will, and the execution and revocation of wills in general.

PROBATE CODE

CHAPTER II. DESCENT AND DISTRIBUTION

§ 37. Passage of Title Upon Intestacy and Under a Will
When a person dies, leaving a lawful will, all of his estate devised or bequeathed by such will, and all powers of appointment granted in such will, shall vest immediately in the devisees or legatees of such estate and the donees of such powers; and all the estate of such person, not devised or bequeathed, shall vest immediately in his heirs at law; subject, however, to the payment of the debts of the testator or intestate, except such as is exempted by law, and subject to the payment of court-ordered child support payments that are delinquent on the date of the person's death; and whenever a person dies intestate, all of his estate shall vest immediately in his heirs at law, but with the exception aforesaid shall still be liable and subject in their hands to the payment of the debts of the intestate and the delinquent child support payments; but upon the issuance of letters testamentary or of administration upon any such estate, the executor or administrator shall have the right to possession of the estate as it existed at the death of the testator or intestate, with the exception aforesaid; and he shall recover possession of and hold such estate in trust to be disposed of in accordance with the law.

CHAPTER IV. EXECUTION AND REVOCATION OF WILLS

§ 58. Interests Which May Pass Under a Will

(a) Every person competent to make a last will and testament may thereby devise and bequeath all the estate, right, title, and interest in property the person has at the time of the person's death, subject to the limitations prescribed by law.

(b) A person who makes a last will and testament may:

(1) disinherit an heir; and

(2) direct the disposition of property or an interest passing under the will or by intestacy.

(c) A legacy of personal property does not include any contents of the property unless the will directs that the contents are included in the legacy. A devise of real property does not include any personal property located on or associated with the real property or any contents of personal property located on the real property unless the will directs that the personal property or contents are included in the devise.

(d) In this section:

(1) "Contents" means tangible personal property, other than titled personal property, found inside of or on a specifically bequeathed or devised item. The term includes clothing, pictures, furniture, coin collections, and other items of tangible personal property that do not require a formal transfer of title and that are located in another item of tangible personal property such as a cedar chest or other furniture.

(2) "Titled personal property" includes all tangible personal property represented by a certificate of title, certificate of ownership, written label, marking, or designation that signifies ownership by a person. The term includes a motor vehicle, motor home, motorboat, or other similar property that requires a formal transfer of title.

§ 59. Requisites of a Will

(a) Every last will and testament, except where otherwise provided by law, shall be in writing and signed by the testator in person or by another person for him by his direction and in his presence, and shall, if not wholly in the handwriting of the testator, be attested by two or more credible witnesses above the age of fourteen years who shall subscribe their names thereto in their own handwriting in the presence of the testator. Such a will or testament may, at the time of its execution or at any subsequent date during the lifetime of the testator and the witnesses, be made self-proved, and the testimony of the witnesses in the probate thereof may be made unnecessary, by the affidavits of the testator and the attesting witnesses, made before an officer authorized to administer oaths under the laws of this State. Provided that nothing shall require an affidavit or certificate of any testator or testatrix as a prerequisite to self-proof of a will or testament other than the certificate set out below. The affidavits shall be evidenced by a certificate, with official seal affixed, of such officer attached or annexed to such will or testament in form and contents substantially as follows:

THE STATE OF TEXAS
COUNTY OF _____
Before me, the undersigned authority, on this day personally appeared _____, _____, and _____, known to me to be the testator and the witnesses, respectively, whose names are subscribed to the annexed or foregoing instrument in their respective capacities, and, all of said persons being by

me duly sworn, the said _____, testator, declared to me and to the said witnesses in my presence that said instrument is his last will and testament, and that he had willingly made and executed it as his free act and deed; and the said witnesses, each on his oath stated to me, in the presence and hearing of the said testator, that the said testator had declared to them that said instrument is his last will and testament, and that he executed same as such and wanted each of them to sign it as a witness; and upon their oaths each witness stated further that they did sign the same as witnesses in the presence of the said testator and at his request; that he was at that time eighteen years of age or over (or being under such age, was or had been lawfully married, or was then a member of the armed forces of the United States or of an auxiliary thereof or of the Maritime Service) and was of sound mind; and that each of said witnesses was then at least fourteen years of age.

_____

Testator

_____

Witness

_____

Witness

Subscribed and sworn to before me by the said _____, testator, and by the said _____ and _____, witnesses, this _____ day of _____ A.D. _____.

(SEAL)
(Signed)_____
(Official Capacity of Officer)
(a) An affidavit in form and content substantially as provided by Subsection (b) of this section is a "self-proving affidavit." A will with a self-proving affidavit subscribed and sworn to by the testator and witnesses attached or annexed to the will is a "self-proved will." Substantial compliance with the form of such affidavit shall suffice to cause the will to be self-proved. For this purpose, an affidavit that is subscribed and acknowledged by the testator and subscribed and sworn to by the witnesses would suffice as being in substantial compliance. A signature on a self-proving affidavit is considered a signature to the will if necessary to prove that the will was signed by the testator or witnesses, or both, but in that case, the will may not be considered a self-proved will.

(c) A self-proved will may be admitted to probate without the testimony of any subscribing witness, but otherwise it shall be treated no differently than a will not self-proved. In particular and without limiting the generality of the foregoing, a self-proved will may be contested, or revoked or amended by a codicil in exactly the same fashion as a will not self-proved.

§ 63. Revocation of Wills
No will in writing, and no clause thereof or devise therein, shall be revoked, except by a subsequent will, codicil, or declaration in writing, executed with like formalities, or by the testator destroying or canceling the same, or causing it to be done in his presence.

Explanation of Federal Estate Taxes, Including Estate and Gift Schedule

As discussed throughout the text, all property you own at your death (probate and nonprobate) is subject to the federal estate tax at your death. The federal estate tax applies to all estates. However, the law grants you a *unified credit* and your estate does not have to pay tax on an amount up to that credit. In 2005, the unified credit is $1,500,000.

Under this law, the estate tax will be completely repealed by the year 2010. The law also reduces the highest estate and gift tax rates. The following table sets forth the increase in the *unified credit* and the decrease in the estate and gift tax rate.

Calendar Year	Estate and Gift Tax Unified Credit Amount	Highest Estate & Gift Tax Rate
2005	$1.5 million	47%
2006	$2 million	46%
2007	$2 million	45%
2008	$2 million	45%
2009	$3.5 million	45%
2010	N/A	Replaced by top individual income tax rate (gifts only)
2011	$1 million	55%

Under the current law, when an individual inherits property and later sells it, the person does not have to pay capital gains tax on the appreciation that occurred prior to the death of the person from whom they inherited the property. The heir is able to *step up* the basis of the asset to the value at the date of the decedent's death. Capital gain is then calculated from the date of death until the date of sale.

In 2010, however, with the repeal of the estate tax, the step-up in rules will change for property inherited from a decedent. A decedent's estate will be permitted to increase the basis of assets transferred to heirs up to a total of $1.3 million. The basis of property transferred to a surviving spouse could be increased by $3.0 million. Thus, the basis of property transferred to a surviving spouse could be increased by a total of $4.3 million.

For anyone who has an estate in excess of $1.3 million, there will still be a tax that will eventually be paid—a capital gains tax—by the beneficiary. The problems will come when executors, trustees, beneficiaries, and their accountants have to determine the decedent's basis in assets to make the proper step-up. There will also be problems later when a beneficiary sells assets that did not receive a step-up in basis upon the decedent's death.

NOTE: *The law provides that there will be no estate tax in the year 2010. It also provides that unless Congress takes action before December 31, 2010, the estate tax will come back into effect. Then, the unified credit exemption will only be $1,000,000 for each decedent.*

Sample, Filled-In Forms

The following pages include sample, filled-in forms for some of the wills in this book. They are filled out in different ways for different situations. You should look at all of them to see how the different sections can be filled in. Only one example of a self-proved will affidavit is shown, but you should use it with every will.

Last Will and Testament

I, _____John Doe_____ a resident of _____Leon_____ County, Texas do hereby make, publish and declare this to be my Last Will and Testament, hereby revoking any and all Wills and Codicils heretofore made by me.

FIRST: I direct that all my just debts and funeral expenses be paid out of my estate as soon after my death as is practicable.

SECOND: I give and bequeath the following personal property unto the following persons:

My gold pocketwatch	to	James Doe
My antique bookcase	to	Sally Doe
--	to	--

THIRD: All the rest, residue and remainder of my estate, real or personal, wheresoever situate, now owned or hereafter acquired by me, which at the time of my death shall belong to me or be subject to my disposal by will, I give, devise and bequeath unto my spouse, _____Mary Doe_____. If my said spouse does not survive me, I give, and bequeath the said property to my children James Doe, Mary Doe, Larry Doe, Barry Doe Carrie Doe, and Moe Doe ---, plus any afterborn or adopted children in equal shares.

FOURTH: In the event that any beneficiary fails to survive me by thirty days, then this will shall take effect as if that person had predeceased me.

FIFTH: Should my spouse not survive me, I hereby nominate, constitute and appoint _____Mary Doe_____, as guardian over the person of any of my children who have not reached the age of majority at the time of my death. In the event that said guardian is unable or unwilling to serve then I nominate, constitute and appoint _____Madeleine Doe_____ as guardian. Said guardian to serve without bond or surety.

SIXTH: Should my spouse not survive me, I hereby nominate, constitute and appoint _____Mary Doe_____ as guardian over the estate of any of my children who have not reached the age of majority at the time of my death. In the event that said guardian is unable or unwilling to serve then I nominate, constitute and appoint _____Englebert Doe_____ as guardian. Said guardian to serve without bond or surety.

SEVENTH: I hereby nominate, constitute and appoint _____Mary Doe_____ to serve as Executor of this, my Last Will and Testament, to serve without bond or surety. In the event that he or she is unable or unwilling to serve at any time or for any reason then I nominate, constitute and appoint _____Englebert Doe_____ as alternate Executor also to serve without bond or surety. I give my said Executor the fullest power in all matters including the power to sell or convey real or personal property or any interest therein without court order. My Executor shall serve as an independent executor, and no action shall be had in the county court in relation to the settlement of my estate other than the probating and recording of my Will and the return of an inventory, appraisement and list of claims of my estate, as provided by law.

IN WITNESS WHEREOF I declare this to be my Last Will and Testament and execute it willingly as my free and voluntary act for the purposes expressed herein and I am of legal age and sound mind and make this under no constraint or undue influence, this ___5th___ day of ___January___, __2006__ .

_____John Doe_____ L.S.

The foregoing instrument was on said date subscribed at the end thereof by _____<u>John Doe</u>_____, the above named Testator who signed, published, and declared this instrument to be his/her Last Will and Testament in the presence of us and each of us, who thereupon at his/her request, in his/her presence, and in the presence of each other, have hereunto subscribed our names as witnesses thereto. We understand this to be his/her will and to the best of our knowledge testator is of legal age, of sound mind and under no constraint or undue influence.

_____Rick Richards_____ residing at _____5432 South Street_____

_____Robert Robinson_____ residing at _____1234 Main Street_____

Last Will and Testament

I, _____Jane Taylor_____ a resident of _____Smith_____ County, Texas do hereby make, publish and declare this to be my Last Will and Testament, hereby revoking any and all Wills and Codicils heretofore made by me.

FIRST: I direct that all my just debts and funeral expenses be paid out of my estate as soon after my death as is practicable.

SECOND: I give and bequeath the following personal property unto the following persons:

My 1 carat diamond wedding ring	to	Judith Jones
My Lenox Collection	to	Sally Smith
---	to	---

THIRD: All the rest, residue and remainder of my estate, real or personal, wheresoever situate, now owned or hereafter acquired by me, which at the time of my death shall belong to me or be subject to my disposal by will, I give, devise and bequeath unto my spouse, _____Michael Taylor_____. If my said spouse does not survive me, I give, and bequeath the said property to my children Judith Jones, Sally Smith, John Taylor, Janet Taylor _____

_____,

plus any afterborn or adopted children in equal shares.

FOURTH: In the event that any beneficiary fails to survive me by thirty days, then this will shall take effect as if that person had predeceased me.

FIFTH: In the event that any of my children have not reached the age of __25__ years at the time of my death, then the share of any such child shall be held IN TRUST by _____John Taylor_____until such time as such child or children reach the age of __25__ years. The trustee shall use the income and that part of the principal of the trust as is, in the discretion of the trustee, necessary or desirable to provide proper housing, medical care, food, clothing, entertainment and education for the trust beneficiaries. In the event the said trustee is unable or unwilling to serve for any reason, then I nominate, constitute and appoint _____Bob Smith_____as alternate trustee. No bond shall be required of either trustee in any jurisdiction.

SIXTH: Should my spouse not survive me, I hereby nominate, constitute and appoint_____Bob Smith_____as guardian over the person and estate of any of my children who have not reached the age of majority at the time of my death. In the event that said guardian is unable or unwilling to serve then I nominate, constitute and appoint_____Robert Jones_____ as guardian.

SEVENTH: I hereby nominate, constitute and appoint _____Michael Taylor_____ to serve as Executor of this, my Last Will and Testament, to serve without bond or surety. In the event that he or she is unable or unwilling to serve at any time or for any reason then I nominate, constitute and appoint _____Bob Smith_____ as alternate Executor also to serve without bond or surety. I give my said Executor the fullest power in all matters including the power to sell or convey real or personal property or any interest therein without court order. My Executor shall serve as an independent executor, and no action shall be had in the county court in relation to the settlement of my estate other than the probating and recording of my Will and the return of an inventory, appraisement and list of claims of my estate, as provided by law.

IN WITNESS WHEREOF I declare this to be my Last Will and Testament and execute it willingly as my free and voluntary act for the purposes expressed herein and I am of legal age and sound mind and make this under no constraint or undue influence, this __7th__ day of _____July_____, __2006__.

Jane Taylor

The foregoing instrument was on said date subscribed at the end thereof by _____Jane Taylor_____, the above named Testator who signed, published, and declared this instrument to be his/her Last Will and Testament in the presence of us and each of us, who thereupon at his/her request, in his/her presence, and in the presence of each other, have hereunto subscribed our names as witnesses thereto. We understand this to be his/her will and to the best of our knowledge testator is of legal age, of sound mind and under no constraint or undue influence.

Henry Roberts residing at 1010 Apple Street, Austin, Texas

Heather Roberts residing at 1010 Apple Street, Austin, Texas

Last Will and Testament

I, _____John Smith_____ a resident of _____Hockley_____ County, Texas do hereby make, publish and declare this to be my Last Will and Testament, hereby revoking any and all Wills and Codicils heretofore made by me.

FIRST: I direct that all my just debts and funeral expenses be paid out of my estate as soon after my death as is practicable.

SECOND: I give and bequeath the following personal property unto the following persons:

My gold pocketwatch	to	_Danny Smith_
My antique bookcase	to	_Sally Smith_
--	to	--

THIRD: All the rest, residue and remainder of my estate, real or personal, wheresoever situate, now owned or hereafter acquired by me, which at the time of my death shall belong to me or be subject to my disposal by will, I give, devise and bequeath unto my spouse, _____Barbara Smith_____. If my said spouse does not survive me, I give, and bequeath the said property to my children _Amy Smith, Beamy Smith and Seamy Smith_ --- ---, in equal shares or to their lineal descendants, per stirpes.

FOURTH: In the event that any beneficiary fails to survive me by thirty days, then this will shall take effect as if that person had predeceased me.

FIFTH: I hereby nominate, constitute and appoint ___Barbara Smith___ to serve as Executor of this, my Last Will and Testament, to serve without bond or surety. In the event that he or she is unable or unwilling to serve at any time or for any reason then I nominate, constitute and appoint ___Reginald Smith___ as alternate Executor also to serve without bond or surety. I give my said Executor the fullest power in all matters including the power to sell or convey real or personal property or any interest therein without court order. My Executor shall serve as an independent executor, and no action shall be had in the county court in relation to the settlement of my estate other than the probating and recording of my Will and the return of an inventory, appraisement and list of claims of my estate, as provided by law.

IN WITNESS WHEREOF I declare this to be my Last Will and Testament and execute it willingly as my free and voluntary act for the purposes expressed herein and I am of legal age and sound mind and make this under no constraint or undue influence, this _5th_ day of _January_, _2006_.

John Smith

Last Will and Testament

I, _____John Doe_____ a resident of ___Leon_____ County, Texas do hereby make, publish and declare this to be my Last Will and Testament, hereby revoking any and all Wills and Codicils heretofore made by me.

FIRST: I direct that all my just debts and funeral expenses be paid out of my estate as soon after my death as is practicable.

SECOND: I give and bequeath the following personal property unto the following persons:

_My gold pocketwatch_____ to _____James Doe_____
_My antique bookcase_____ to _____Sally Doe_____
_____ to _____

THIRD: All the rest, residue and remainder of my estate, real or personal, wheresoever situate, now owned or hereafter acquired by me, which at the time of my death shall belong to me or be subject to my disposal by will, I give, devise and bequeath unto my children _James Doe, Mary Doe, Larry Doe, Barry Doe, Carrie Doe, and Moe Doe_------------------ -- --, plus any afterborn or adopted children in equal shares or to their lineal descendants per stirpes.

FOURTH: In the event that any beneficiary fails to survive me by thirty days, then this will shall take effect as if that person had predeceased me.

FIFTH: In the event that any of my children have not reached the age of __25___ years at the time of my death, then the share of any such child shall be held IN TRUST by _____James Doe_____until such time as such child or children reach the age of __25___ years. The trustee shall use the income and that part of the principal of the trust as is, in the discretion of the trustee, necessary or desirable to provide proper housing, medical care, food, clothing, entertainment and education for the trust beneficiaries. In the event the said trustee is unable or unwilling to serve for any reason, then I nominate, constitute and appoint _____Sally Doe_____as alternate trustee. No bond shall be required of either trustee in any jurisdiction.

SIXTH: In the event any of my children have not attained the age of 18 years at the time of my death, I hereby nominate, constitute and appoint _____Sally Doe_____ as guardian over the property of any of my children who have not reached the age of majority at the time of my death. In the event that said guardian is unable or unwilling to serve then I nominate, constitute and appoint _____Madeleine Small_____ as guardian. Said guardian to serve without bond or surety.

SEVENTH: I hereby nominate, constitute and appoint _____James Doe_____ to serve as Executor of this, my Last Will and Testament, to serve without bond or surety. In the event that he or she is unable or unwilling to serve at any time or for any reason then I nominate, constitute and appoint _____Englebert Doe_____ as alternate Executor also to serve without bond or surety. I give my said Executor the fullest power in all matters including the power to sell or convey real or personal property or any interest therein without court order. My Executor shall serve as an independent executor, and no action shall be had in the county court in relation to the settlement of my estate other than the probating and recording of my Will and the return of an inventory, appraisement and list of claims of my estate, as provided by law.

IN WITNESS WHEREOF I declare this to be my Last Will and Testament and execute it willingly as my free and voluntary act for the purposes expressed herein and I am of legal age and sound mind and make this under no constraint or undue influence, this ___5th___ day of _January_____, __2006__ .

_____ *John Doe* _____

The foregoing instrument was on said date subscribed at the end thereof by _____ John Doe _____ , the above named Testator who signed, published, and declared this instrument to be his/her Last Will and Testament in the presence of us and each of us, who thereupon at his/her request, in his/her presence, and in the presence of each other, have hereunto subscribed our names as witnesses thereto. We understand this to be his/her will and to the best of our knowledge testator is of legal age, of sound mind and under no constraint or undue influence.

_____ *Rick Richards* _____ residing at _____ 5432 South Street _____

_____ *Robert Robinson* _____ residing at _____ 1234 Main Street _____

Last Will and Testament

I, _____John Smith_____ a resident of ____Hockely____ County, Texas do hereby make, publish and declare this to be my Last Will and Testament, hereby revoking any and all Wills and Codicils heretofore made by me.

FIRST: I direct that all my just debts and funeral expenses be paid out of my estate as soon after my death as is practicable.

SECOND: I give and bequeath the following personal property unto the following persons:

_My gold pocketwatch_____ to _____Danny Smith_____

_My antique bookcase_____ to _____Sally Smith_____

_____ to _____

THIRD: All the rest, residue and remainder of my estate, real or personal, wheresoever situate, now owned or hereafter acquired by me, which at the time of my death shall belong to me or be subject to my disposal by will, I give, devise and bequeath unto the following _75% to my dear friend, Frannie Farkle, or her lineal descendants, per stirpes; 15%_ _to the Hockley County Humane Society; 10% to Texas Tech. University_____ _____, ~~in equal shares, or their lineal descendants per stirpes.~~

FOURTH: In the event that any beneficiary fails to survive me by thirty days, then this will shall take effect as if that person had predeceased me.

FIFTH: I hereby nominate, constitute and appoint __Frannie Farkle__ to serve as Executor of this, my Last Will and Testament, to serve without bond or surety. In the event that he or she is unable or unwilling to serve at any time or for any reason then I nominate, constitute and appoint ____Danny Smith____ as alternate Executor also to serve without bond or surety. I give my said Executor the fullest power in all matters including the power to sell or convey real or personal property or any interest therein without court order. My Executor shall serve as an independent executor, and no action shall be had in the county court in relation to the settlement of my estate other than the probating and recording of my Will and the return of an inventory, appraisement and list of claims of my estate, as provided by law.

IN WITNESS WHEREOF I declare this to be my Last Will and Testament and execute it willingly as my free and voluntary act for the purposes expressed herein and I am of legal age and sound mind and make this under no constraint or undue influence, this _29th_ day of _January_____, _2006_.

_____*John Smith*_____

Self-Proving Affidavit

STATE OF TEXAS   §
                            §

COUNTY OF _____Eldorado_____   §

      BEFORE ME, the undersigned authority, on this day personally appeared _____John Doe_____, _____Melvin Coe_____ and _____Jane Roe_____, known to me to be the Testator and the witnesses, respectively, whose names are subscribed to the annexed or foregoing instrument in their respective capacities; and all of said persons being by me duly sworn, the Testator declared to me and to the witnesses in my presence that said instrument is his/her Will, and that he/she had willingly made and executed it as his/her free act and deed for the purposes therein expressed; and the witnesses, each on his oath, stated to me in the presence and hearing of the Testator that the Testator had declared to them that said instrument is his/her Will, and that he/she executed same as such and wanted each of them to sign it as a witness; and upon their oaths each witness stated further that they did sign the same as witnesses in the presence of the Testator and at his/her request, that he/she was at that time eighteen (18) years of age or over and was of sound mind, and that each of the witnesses was then at least fourteen (14) years of age.

John Doe
_____
TESTATOR

Jane Roe
_____
WITNESS

Melvin Coe
_____
WITNESS

SUBSCRIBED AND ACKNOWLEDGED before me by _____John Doe_____, the Testator and subscribed and sworn to before me by the above-named witnesses this _____5th_____ day of _____July_____, 2006 .

C. U. Sine
_____
Notary Public

First Codicil to the Will of
<u>Larry Lowe</u>

I, <u>Larry Lowe</u>, a resident of <u>Eldorado</u> County, Texas declare this to be the first codicil to my Last Will and Testament dated <u>July 5</u>, <u>2005</u>.

FIRST: I hereby revoke the clause of my Will which reads as follows: _____
<u>FOURTH: I hereby leave $5,000.00 to my daughter Mildred Lowe</u>
_____
_____

SECOND: I hereby add following clause to my Will: _____
<u>FOURTH: I hereby leave $1,000.00 to my daughter Mildred Lowe</u>
_____
_____

THIRD: In all other respects I hereby confirm and republish my Last Will and Testament dated <u>July 5</u>, <u>2005</u>.

Date: <u>January 15, 2006</u>   *Larry Lowe*

We, the undersigned persons, of lawful age, have on this <u>5th</u> day of <u>January</u>, <u>2006</u>, at the request of <u>Larry Lowe</u>, witnessed his/her signature to the foregoing First Codicil to Will in the presence of each of us; and we have, at the same time and in his/her presence and in the presence of each other, subscribed our names hereto as attesting witnesses.

Michael Smith   residing at: <u>21 Oak Lane</u>
                                 <u>Ft. Worth, TX 76011</u>
Mary Smith   residing at: <u>121 Wall Street</u>
                                 <u>Ft. Worth, TX 76102</u>

SELF-PROVING AFFIDAVIT

STATE OF TEXAS   §
                             §
COUNTY OF <u>Eldorado</u>   §

BEFORE ME, the undersigned authority, on this day personally appeared <u>Larry Lowe</u>, <u>Michael Smith</u>, and <u>Mary Smith</u>, known to me to be the Testator and the witnesses, respectively, whose names are subscribed to the annexed or foregoing instrument in their respective capacities; and all of said persons being by me duly sworn, the Testator declared to me and to the witnesses in my presence that said instrument is his/her First Codicil to Will, and that he/she had willingly made and executed it as his/her free act and deed for the purposes therein expressed; and the witnesses, each on his oath, stated to me in the presence and hearing of the Testator that the Testator had declared to them that said instrument is his/her First Codicil to Will, and that he/she executed same as such and wanted each of them to sign it as a witness; and upon their oaths each witness stated further that they did sign the same as witnesses in the presence of the Testator and at his/her request, that he/she was at that time eighteen (18) years of age or over and was of sound mind, and that each of the witnesses was then at least fourteen (14) years of age.

Larry Lowe   *Michael Smith*
TESTATOR   WITNESS

                                      Mary Smith
                                      WITNESS

SUBSCRIBED AND ACKNOWLEDGED before me by <u>Larry Lowe</u>, the Testator and subscribed and sworn to before me by the above-named witnesses this <u>5th</u> day of <u>January</u>, <u>2006</u>.

                                      Arthur Izer
                                      Notary Public

Page <u>1</u> of <u>1</u>

Advance Directive

I, _____John Doe_____, recognize that the best health care is based upon a partnership of trust and communication with my physician. My physician and I will make health care decisions together as long as I am of sound mind and able to make my wishes known. If there comes a time that I am unable to make medical decisions about myself because of illness or injury, I direct that the following treatment preferences be honored:

If, in the judgment of my physician, I am suffering with a terminal condition from which I am expected to die within six months, even with available life-sustaining treatment provided in accordance with prevailing standards of medical care:

___JD___   I request that all treatments other than those needed to keep me comfortable be discontinued or withheld and my physician allow me to die as gently as possible; OR

_____   I request that I be kept alive in this terminal condition using available life-sustaining treatment. (THIS SELECTION DOES NOT APPLY TO HOSPICE CARE.)

If, in the judgment of my physician, I am suffering with an irreversible condition so that I cannot care for myself or make decisions for myself and am expected to die without life-sustaining treatment provided in accordance with prevailing standards of medical care:

___JD___   I request that all treatment other than those needed to keep me comfortable be discontinued or withheld and my physician allow me to die as gently as possible; OR

_____   I request that I be kept alive in this irreversible condition using available life-sustaining treatment. (THIS SELECTION DOES NOT APPLY TO HOSPICE CARE.)

Additional requests: (After discussion with your physician, you may wish to consider listing particular treatments in this space that you do or do not want in specific circumstances, such as artificial nutrition and fluids, intravenous antibiotics, etc. Be sure to state whether you do or do not want the particular treatment.)

_____

_____

After signing this directive, if my representative or I elect hospice care, I understand and agree that only those treatments needed to keep me comfortable would be provided and I would not be given available life-sustaining treatments.

If I do not have a Medical Power of Attorney, and I am unable to make my wishes known, I designate the following person(s) to make treatment decisions with my physician compatible with my personal values:

1. _____

2. _____

(If a Medical Power of Attorney has been executed, than an agent already has been named and you should not list additional names in this document.)

If the above persons are not available, or if I have not designated a spokesperson, I understand that a spokesperson will be chosen for me following standards specified in the laws of Texas. If, in the judgment of my physician, my death is imminent within minutes to hours, even with the use of all available medical treatment provided within the prevailing standard of care, I acknowledge that all treatments may be withheld or removed except those needed to maintain my comfort. I understand that under Texas law this directive has no effect if I have been diagnosed as pregnant. This directive will remain in effect until I revoke it. No other person may do so.

Signed this ___12th___ day of _____October_____ , _2006_ , in ___San Antonio___ , _____Bexar_____ County, Texas.

John Doe

[Print Name]: _John Doe_

The witnesses acknowledge that the declarant signed this directive in their presence and that each of them is over the age of eighteen (18) years and competent to witness this document. The witness designated at "Witness 1" is: (1) not a person designated by the declarant to make a treatment decision for the declarant; (2) not related to the declarant by blood or marriage; (3) not entitled to any portion of the declarant's estate on declarant's death; (4) not a claimant against the estate of the declarant; (5) not the attending physician or employee of the attending physician of declarant; and (6) not an officer, director, partner, or business office employee of a health care facility in which the declarant is being cared for or of any parent organization of the health care facility. Furthermore, if "Witness 1" is an employee of a health care facility in which the declarant is a patient, such witness is not involved in providing direct patient care to the declarant.

Richard Anderson
Witness 1
Address: _35 Cedar Street_
San Antonio, Texas

Sally Jones
Witness 2
Address: _123 Main Street_
San Antonio, Texas

MEDICAL POWER OF ATTORNEY
AND DESIGNATION OF HEALTH CARE AGENT

1.   DESIGNATION OF HEALTH CARE AGENT

I, _____ Mary Smith _____ , appoint:

Name: Michael Smith
Address: 55 Elm Avenue
           Houston, Texas
Phone: (713) 333-1211

as my agent to make any and all health care decisions for me, except to the extent I state otherwise in this document. This Medical Power of Attorney takes effect if I become unable to make my own health care decisions and this fact is certified in writing by my physician.

LIMITATIONS ON THE DECISION MAKING AUTHORITY OF MY AGENT ARE AS FOLLOWS:
NONE

2.   DESIGNATION OF ALTERNATE AGENT

(You are not required to designate an alternate agent but you may do so. An alternate agent may make the same health care decisions as the designated agent if the designated agent is unable or unwilling to act as your agent. If the agent designated is your spouse, the designation is automatically revoked by law if your marriage is dissolved).

If the person designated as my agent is unable or unwilling to make health care decisions for me, I designate the following person to serve as my agent to make health care decisions for me as authorized by this document:

First Alternate Agent

Name: Susan Johnson
Address: 1367 Riverside Way
           Dallas, Texas
Phone: (214) 498-5601

Page 1 of 3

Second Alternate Agent

Name: NOT APPLICABLE _____

Address: _____

               _____

Phone: _____

An original of this document is kept at:

           666 Holley Lane _____

           San Antonio, Texas _____

The following individuals or institutions have signed copies:

Name: Michael Smith _____

Address: 55 Elm Avenue _____

               Houston, Texas _____

Phone: (713) 333-1211 _____

Name: Susan Johnson _____

Address: 1367 Riverside Way _____

               Dallas, Texas _____

Phone: (214) 498-5601 _____

3.   **DURATION**

I understand that this Medical Power of Attorney exists indefinitely from the date I execute this document unless I establish a shorter time or revoke the power of attorney. If I am unable to make health care decisions for myself when this power of attorney expires, the authority I have granted my agent continues to exist until the time I become able to make health care decisions for myself.

(IF APPLICABLE) This Medical Power of Attorney ends on the following date:

_____

4.   **PRIOR DESIGNATIONS REVOKED**

I revoke any prior Medical Power of Attorney.

5. ACKNOWLEDGMENT OF DISCLOSURE STATEMENT

I have been provided with a disclosure statement explaining the effect of this document. I have read and understand that information contained in the disclosure statement.

(YOU MUST DATE AND SIGN THIS POWER OF ATTORNEY.)

I sign my name to this Medical Power of Attorney on the ___12th___ day of _____October_____, 20 _06_ , at _____San Antonio_____, _____Bexar_____ County, Texas.

Mary Smith
Print Name: __Mary Smith__

STATEMENT AND SIGNATURE OF FIRST WITNESS:

I am not the person appointed as agent by this document. I am not related to the principal by blood or marriage. I would not be entitled to any portion of the principal's estate on the principal's death. I am not the attending physician of the principal or an employee of the attending physician. I have no claim against any portion of the principals estate on the principal's death. Furthermore, if I am an employee of a health care facility in which the principal is a patient, I am not involved in providing direct patient care to the principal and am not an officer, director, partner, or business office employee of the health care facility or of any parent organization of the health care facility.

Witness Signature: *Sally Jones*
Print Name: __Sally Jones__ Date: October 12, 2006
Address: __123 Main Street, San Antonio, Texas__

SIGNATURE OF SECOND WITNESS:

Witness Signature: *Richard Anderson*
Print Name: __Richard Anderson__ Date: October 12, 2006
Address: __35 Cedar Street, San Antonio, Texas__

Blank Forms

The following pages contain forms that can be used to prepare a will, codicil, directive to physicians, and organ donor card. They should only be used by persons who have read this book, who do not have any complications in their legal affairs, and who understand the forms they are using. The forms may be used right out of the book or downloaded from the accompanying CD-ROM.

This form is used to spell out your wishes for donation of your body or any organs and can be carried in your wallet or purse.

How to Pick the Right Will

Follow the chart and use the form number in the black circle—
then use form 19, the self-proving affidavit.

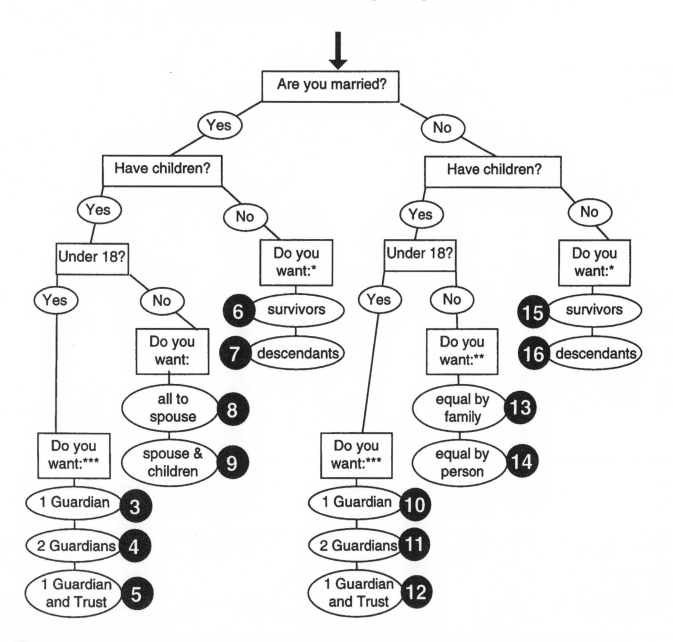

17 Be sure to use form 19, the self-proving affidavit with your will, no matter which form you use.

* For an explanation of survivors/descendants, see page 34.

** For an explanation of families/persons, see page 33.

*** For an explanation of children's guardians and trust, see pages 35 and 36.

This page intentionally blank.

Asset and Beneficiary List

Property Inventory

Assets

Bank Accounts (checking, savings, certificates of deposit)

_____
_____
_____
_____
_____
_____
_____

Real Estate

_____
_____
_____
_____
_____
_____
_____
_____

Vehicles (cars, trucks, boats, planes, RVs, etc.)

_____
_____
_____
_____
_____
_____
_____
_____

Personal Property (collections, jewelry, tools, artwork, household items, etc.)

_____
_____
_____
_____
_____
_____
_____
_____
_____

_____
_____
_____
_____
_____

Stocks/Bonds/Mutual Funds

_____
_____
_____
_____
_____
_____
_____
_____
_____
_____
_____
_____
_____

Retirement Accounts (IRAs, 401(k)s, pension plans, etc.)

_____
_____
_____
_____
_____
_____
_____

Receivables (mortgages held, notes, accounts receivable, personal loans)

_____
_____
_____
_____
_____
_____
_____

Life Insurance

_____
_____
_____
_____
_____
_____
_____
_____

Other property (trusts, partnerships, businesses, profit sharing, copyrights, etc.)

_____
_____
_____
_____
_____
_____
_____
_____

Liabilities

Real Estate Loans

_____
_____
_____
_____
_____
_____
_____
_____

Vehicle Loans

_____
_____
_____
_____
_____
_____
_____
_____

Other Secured Loans

_____
_____
_____
_____
_____
_____
_____
_____

Unsecured Loans and Debts (taxes, child support, judgments, etc.)

_____
_____
_____
_____
_____
_____
_____
_____

Beneficiary List

Name _____ Address _____ Phone _____

_____
_____
_____
_____
_____
_____
_____

Preferences List

STATEMENT OF DESIRES AND LOCATION OF PROPERTY & DOCUMENTS

I, _____, am signing this document as the expression of my desires as to the matters stated below, and to inform my family members or other significant persons of the location of certain property and documents in the event of any emergency or of my death.

1. **Funeral Desires.** It is my desire that the following arrangements be made for my funeral and disposition of remains in the event of my death (state if you have made any arrangements, such as prepaid burial plans, cemetery plots owned, etc.):

    ❏   Burial at _____
        _____.

    ❏   Cremation at _____
        _____.

    ❏   Other specific desires: _____
        _____
        _____.

2. **Pets.** I have the following pet(s): _____

The following are my desires concerning the care of said pet(s): _____
_____
_____
_____

3. **Notification.** I would like the following person(s) notified in the event of emergency or death (give name, address and phone number):

_____
_____
_____
_____
_____

4. **Location of Documents.** The following is a list of important documents, and their location:

    ❏   Last Will and Testament, dated _____. Location: _____
        _____.

    ❏   Durable Power of Attorney, dated _____. Location: _____
        _____.

    ❏   Living Will, dated _____. Location: _____
        _____.

    ❏   Deed(s) to real estate (describe property location and location of deed):
        _____
        _____
        _____

❑ Title(s) to vehicles (cars, boats, etc.) (describe vehicle, its location, and location of title, registration, or other documents):

_____
_____
_____
_____

❑ Life insurance policies (list name address & phone number of insurance company and insurance agent, policy number, and location of policy):

_____
_____
_____

❑ Other insurance policies (list type, company & agent, policy number, and location of policy):

_____
_____
_____

❑ Other (list other documents such as stock certificates, bonds, certificates of deposit, etc., and their location):

_____
_____
_____

5. **Location of Assets.** In addition to items readily visible in my home or listed above, I have the following assets:

❑ Safe-deposit box located at _____, box number _____. Key located at: _____.

❑ Bank accounts (list name & address of bank, type of account, and account number):

_____

❑ Other (describe the item and give its location):

_____
_____
_____
_____
_____

6. Other desires or information (state any desires or provide any information not given above; use additional sheets of paper if necessary):

_____
_____
_____
_____
_____

Dated: _____   _____
                                                      Signature

List of Important Advisors

_____ PHONE: _____
DOCTOR

_____ PHONE: _____
CLERGYMAN

_____ PHONE: _____
EMPLOYER

_____ PHONE: _____
BUSINESS PARTNER

_____ PHONE: _____
ATTORNEY

_____ PHONE: _____
ACCOUNTANT

_____ PHONE: _____
BANKER

_____ PHONE: _____
GENERAL INSURANCE AGENT

_____ PHONE: _____
LIFE INSURANCE AGENT

_____ PHONE: _____
FINANCIAL ADVISOR

_____ PHONE: _____
STOCKBROKER

_____ PHONE: _____
LANDLORD/MORTGAGE HOLDER

_____ PHONE: _____
OTHER

_____ PHONE: _____
OTHER

This page intentionally blank.

List of Emergency Information

NAME: _____ DATE OF BIRTH: _____
SOCIAL SECURITY NUMBER: _____
SPOUSE: _____
ADDRESS: _____
TELEPHONE: _____
DATE OF MARRIAGE: _____
EMPLOYER: _____
EMPLOYER'S ADDRESS: _____

CHILDREN:

NAME: _____ DATE OF BIRTH: _____
ADDRESS: _____

NAME: _____ DATE OF BIRTH: _____
ADDRESS: _____

NAME: _____ DATE OF BIRTH: _____
ADDRESS: _____

NAME: _____ DATE OF BIRTH: _____
ADDRESS: _____

NAME: _____ DATE OF BIRTH: _____
ADDRESS: _____

RELATIVES & FRIENDS:

NAME: _____
ADDRESS: _____

NAME: _____
ADDRESS: _____

NAME: _____
ADDRESS: _____

NAME: _____
ADDRESS: _____

NAME: _____
ADDRESS: _____

This page intentionally blank.

Last Will and Testament

I, _____ a resident of _____ County, Texas do hereby make, publish and declare this to be my Last Will and Testament, hereby revoking any and all Wills and Codicils heretofore made by me.

FIRST: I direct that all my just debts and funeral expenses be paid out of my estate as soon after my death as is practicable.

SECOND: I give and bequeath the following personal property unto the following persons:

_____ to _____

_____ to _____

_____ to _____

THIRD: All the rest, residue and remainder of my estate, real or personal, wheresoever situate, now owned or hereafter acquired by me, which at the time of my death shall belong to me or be subject to my disposal by will, I give, devise and bequeath unto my spouse, _____. If my said spouse does not survive me, I give, and bequeath the said property to my children

_____

_____

_____, plus any afterborn or adopted children in equal shares.

FOURTH: In the event that any beneficiary fails to survive me by thirty days, then this will shall take effect as if that person had predeceased me.

FIFTH: Should my spouse not survive me, I hereby nominate, constitute and appoint _____ as guardian over the person and estate of any of my children who have not reached the age of majority at the time of my death. In the event that said guardian is unable or unwilling to serve then I nominate, constitute and appoint _____ as guardian. Said guardian to serve without bond or surety.

SIXTH: I hereby nominate, constitute and appoint _____ to serve as Executor of this, my Last Will and Testament, to serve without bond or surety. In the event that he or she is unable or unwilling to serve at any time or for any reason then I nominate, constitute and appoint _____ as alternate Executor also to serve without bond or surety. I give my said Executor the fullest power in all matters including the power to sell or convey real or personal property or any interest therein without court order. My Executor shall serve as an independent executor, and no action shall be had in the county court in relation to the settlement of my estate other than the probating and recording of my Will and the return of an inventory, appraisement and list of claims of my estate, as provided by law.

IN WITNESS WHEREOF I declare this to be my Last Will and Testament and execute it willingly as my free and voluntary act for the purposes expressed herein and I am of legal age and sound mind and make this under no constraint or undue influence, this _____ day of _____, _____.

_____

The foregoing instrument was on said date subscribed at the end thereof by _____, the above named Testator who signed, published, and declared this instrument to be his/her Last Will and Testament in the presence of us and each of us, who thereupon at his/her request, in his/her presence, and in the presence of each other, have hereunto subscribed our names as witnesses thereto. We understand this to be his/her will and to the best of our knowledge testator is of legal age, of sound mind and under no constraint or undue influence.

_____ residing at _____

_____ residing at _____

Last Will and Testament

I, _____ a resident of _____ County, Texas do hereby make, publish and declare this to be my Last Will and Testament, hereby revoking any and all Wills and Codicils heretofore made by me.

FIRST: I direct that all my just debts and funeral expenses be paid out of my estate as soon after my death as is practicable.

SECOND: I give and bequeath the following personal property unto the following persons:

_____ to _____

_____ to _____

_____ to _____

THIRD: All the rest, residue and remainder of my estate, real or personal, wheresoever situate, now owned or hereafter acquired by me, which at the time of my death shall belong to me or be subject to my disposal by will, I give, devise and bequeath unto my spouse, _____. If my said spouse does not survive me, I give, and bequeath the said property to my children

_____

_____

_____, plus any afterborn or adopted children in equal shares.

FOURTH: In the event that any beneficiary fails to survive me by thirty days, then this will shall take effect as if that person had predeceased me.

FIFTH: Should my spouse not survive me, I hereby nominate, constitute and appoint _____, as guardian over the person of any of my children who have not reached the age of majority at the time of my death. In the event that said guardian is unable or unwilling to serve then I nominate, constitute and appoint _____ as guardian. Said guardian to serve without bond or surety.

SIXTH: Should my spouse not survive me, I hereby nominate, constitute and appoint _____ as guardian over the estate of any of my children who have not reached the age of majority at the time of my death. In the event that said guardian is unable or unwilling to serve then I nominate, constitute and appoint _____ as guardian. Said guardian to serve without bond or surety.

SEVENTH: I hereby nominate, constitute and appoint _____ to serve as Executor of this, my Last Will and Testament, to serve without bond or surety. In the event that he or she is unable or unwilling to serve at any time or for any reason then I nominate, constitute and appoint _____ as alternate Executor also to serve without bond or surety. I give my said Executor the fullest power in all matters including the power to sell or convey real or personal property or any interest therein without court order. My Executor shall serve as an independent executor, and no action shall be had in the county court in relation to the settlement of my estate other than the probating and recording of my Will and the return of an inventory, appraisement and list of claims of my estate, as provided by law.

IN WITNESS WHEREOF I declare this to be my Last Will and Testament and execute it willingly as my free and voluntary act for the purposes expressed herein and I am of legal age and sound mind and make this under no constraint or undue influence, this _____ day of _____, _____.

_____

The foregoing instrument was on said date subscribed at the end thereof by _____, the above named Testator who signed, published, and declared this instrument to be his/her Last Will and Testament in the presence of us and each of us, who thereupon at his/her request, in his/her presence, and in the presence of each other, have hereunto subscribed our names as witnesses thereto. We understand this to be his/her will and to the best of our knowledge testator is of legal age, of sound mind and under no constraint or undue influence.

_____ residing at _____

_____ residing at _____

Last Will and Testament

I, _____ a resident of _____
County, Texas do hereby make, publish and declare this to be my Last Will and
Testament, hereby revoking any and all Wills and Codicils heretofore made by me.

FIRST: I direct that all my just debts and funeral expenses be paid out of my
estate as soon after my death as is practicable.

SECOND: I give and bequeath the following personal property unto the following
persons:

_____ to _____

_____ to _____

_____ to _____

THIRD: All the rest, residue and remainder of my estate, real or personal,
wheresoever situate, now owned or hereafter acquired by me, which at the time of my
death shall belong to me or be subject to my disposal by will, I give, devise and
bequeath unto my spouse, _____. If my said
spouse does not survive me, I give, and bequeath the said property to my children

_____

_____

_____, plus any afterborn or adopted children in equal shares.

FOURTH: In the event that any beneficiary fails to survive me by thirty days,
then this will shall take effect as if that person had predeceased me.

FIFTH: In the event that any of my children have not reached the age of _____
years at the time of my death, then the share of any such child shall be held IN TRUST
by _____until such time as such child or children reach
the age of _____ years. The trustee shall use the income and that part of the principal
of the trust as is, in the discretion of the trustee, necessary or desirable to provide proper
housing, medical care, food, clothing, entertainment and education for the trust beneficiaries. In the event the said trustee is unable or unwilling to serve for any reason, then
I nominate, constitute and appoint _____as alter-
nate trustee. No bond shall be required of either trustee in any jurisdiction.

SIXTH: Should my spouse not survive me, I hereby nominate, constitute and
appoint_____as guardian over the person and estate
of any of my children who have not reached the age of majority at the time of my death.
In the event that said guardian is unable or unwilling to serve then I nominate, constitute and appoint_____ as guardian.

Page _____ of _____

SEVENTH: I hereby nominate, constitute and appoint _____ to serve as Executor of this, my Last Will and Testament, to serve without bond or surety. In the event that he or she is unable or unwilling to serve at any time or for any reason then I nominate, constitute and appoint _____ as alternate Executor also to serve without bond or surety. I give my said Executor the fullest power in all matters including the power to sell or convey real or personal property or any interest therein without court order. My Executor shall serve as an independent executor, and no action shall be had in the county court in relation to the settlement of my estate other than the probating and recording of my Will and the return of an inventory, appraisement and list of claims of my estate, as provided by law.

IN WITNESS WHEREOF I declare this to be my Last Will and Testament and execute it willingly as my free and voluntary act for the purposes expressed herein and I am of legal age and sound mind and make this under no constraint or undue influence, this _____ day of _____, _____.

_____

The foregoing instrument was on said date subscribed at the end thereof by _____, the above named Testator who signed, published, and declared this instrument to be his/her Last Will and Testament in the presence of us and each of us, who thereupon at his/her request, in his/her presence, and in the presence of each other, have hereunto subscribed our names as witnesses thereto. We understand this to be his/her will and to the best of our knowledge testator is of legal age, of sound mind and under no constraint or undue influence.

_____residing at_____

_____residing at_____

Last Will and Testament

I, _____ a resident of _____
County, Texas do hereby make, publish and declare this to be my Last Will and Testament, hereby revoking any and all Wills and Codicils heretofore made by me.

FIRST: I direct that all my just debts and funeral expenses be paid out of my estate as soon after my death as is practicable.

SECOND: I give and bequeath the following personal property unto the following persons:

_____ to _____

_____ to _____

_____ to _____

THIRD: All the rest, residue and remainder of my estate, real or personal, wheresoever situate, now owned or hereafter acquired by me, which at the time of my death shall belong to me or be subject to my disposal by will, I give, devise and bequeath unto my spouse, _____.
If my said spouse does not survive me, I give, and bequeath the said property to

_____

_____

_____, or the survivor of them.

FOURTH: In the event that any beneficiary fails to survive me by thirty days, then this will shall take effect as if that person had predeceased me.

FIFTH: I hereby nominate, constitute and appoint _____ to serve as Executor of this, my Last Will and Testament, to serve without bond or surety. In the event that he or she is unable or unwilling to serve at any time or for any reason then I nominate, constitute and appoint _____ as alternate Executor also to serve without bond or surety. I give my said Executor the fullest power in all matters including the power to sell or convey real or personal property or any interest therein without court order. My Executor shall serve as an independent executor, and no action shall be had in the county court in relation to the settlement of my estate other than the probating and recording of my Will and the return of an inventory, appraisement and list of claims of my estate, as provided by law.

IN WITNESS WHEREOF I declare this to be my Last Will and Testament and execute it willingly as my free and voluntary act for the purposes expressed herein and I am of legal age and sound mind and make this under no constraint or undue influence, this _____ day of _____, _____.

_____

The foregoing instrument was on said date subscribed at the end thereof by _____, the above named Testator who signed, published, and declared this instrument to be his/her Last Will and Testament in the presence of us and each of us, who thereupon at his/her request, in his/her presence, and in the presence of each other, have hereunto subscribed our names as witnesses thereto. We understand this to be his/her will and to the best of our knowledge testator is of legal age, of sound mind and under no constraint or undue influence.

_____residing at_____

_____residing at_____

Last Will and Testament

I, _____ a resident of _____ County, Texas do hereby make, publish and declare this to be my Last Will and Testament, hereby revoking any and all Wills and Codicils heretofore made by me.

FIRST: I direct that all my just debts and funeral expenses be paid out of my estate as soon after my death as is practicable.

SECOND: I give and bequeath the following personal property unto the following persons:

_____ to _____

_____ to _____

_____ to _____

THIRD: All the rest, residue and remainder of my estate, real or personal, wheresoever situate, now owned or hereafter acquired by me, which at the time of my death shall belong to me or be subject to my disposal by will, I give, devise and bequeath unto my spouse, _____.
If my said spouse does not survive me, I give, and bequeath the said property to

_____

_____

_____, or to their lineal descendants, per stirpes.

FOURTH: In the event that any beneficiary fails to survive me by thirty days, then this will shall take effect as if that person had predeceased me.

FIFTH: I hereby nominate, constitute and appoint _____ to serve as Executor of this, my Last Will and Testament, to serve without bond or surety. In the event that he or she is unable or unwilling to serve at any time or for any reason then I nominate, constitute and appoint _____ as alternate Executor also to serve without bond or surety. I give my said Executor the fullest power in all matters including the power to sell or convey real or personal property or any interest therein without court order. My Executor shall serve as an independent executor, and no action shall be had in the county court in relation to the settlement of my estate other than the probating and recording of my Will and the return of an inventory, appraisement and list of claims of my estate, as provided by law.

IN WITNESS WHEREOF I declare this to be my Last Will and Testament and execute it willingly as my free and voluntary act for the purposes expressed herein and I am of legal age and sound mind and make this under no constraint or undue influence, this _____ day of _____, _____.

_____

The foregoing instrument was on said date subscribed at the end thereof by _____, the above named Testator who signed, published, and declared this instrument to be his/her Last Will and Testament in the presence of us and each of us, who thereupon at his/her request, in his/her presence, and in the presence of each other, have hereunto subscribed our names as witnesses thereto. We understand this to be his/her will and to the best of our knowledge testator is of legal age, of sound mind and under no constraint or undue influence.

_____residing at_____

_____residing at_____

Last Will and Testament

I, _____ a resident of _____ County, Texas do hereby make, publish and declare this to be my Last Will and Testament, hereby revoking any and all Wills and Codicils heretofore made by me.

FIRST: I direct that all my just debts and funeral expenses be paid out of my estate as soon after my death as is practicable.

SECOND: I give and bequeath the following personal property unto the following persons:

_____ to _____

_____ to _____

_____ to _____

THIRD: All the rest, residue and remainder of my estate, real or personal, wheresoever situate, now owned or hereafter acquired by me, which at the time of my death shall belong to me or be subject to my disposal by will, I give, devise and bequeath unto my spouse, _____. If my said spouse does not survive me, I give, and bequeath the said property to my children

_____

_____

_____, in equal shares or to their lineal descendants, per stirpes.

FOURTH: In the event that any beneficiary fails to survive me by thirty days, then this will shall take effect as if that person had predeceased me.

FIFTH: I hereby nominate, constitute and appoint _____ to serve as Executor of this, my Last Will and Testament, to serve without bond or surety. In the event that he or she is unable or unwilling to serve at any time or for any reason then I nominate, constitute and appoint _____ as alternate Executor also to serve without bond or surety. I give my said Executor the fullest power in all matters including the power to sell or convey real or personal property or any interest therein without court order. My Executor shall serve as an independent executor, and no action shall be had in the county court in relation to the settlement of my estate other than the probating and recording of my Will and the return of an inventory, appraisement and list of claims of my estate, as provided by law.

IN WITNESS WHEREOF I declare this to be my Last Will and Testament and execute it willingly as my free and voluntary act for the purposes expressed herein and I am of legal age and sound mind and make this under no constraint or undue influence, this _____ day of _____, _____.

_____

The foregoing instrument was on said date subscribed at the end thereof by _____, the above named Testator who signed, published, and declared this instrument to be his/her Last Will and Testament in the presence of us and each of us, who thereupon at his/her request, in his/her presence, and in the presence of each other, have hereunto subscribed our names as witnesses thereto. We understand this to be his/her will and to the best of our knowledge testator is of legal age, of sound mind and under no constraint or undue influence.

_____residing at_____

_____residing at_____

Last Will and Testament

I, _____ a resident of _____ County, Texas do hereby make, publish and declare this to be my Last Will and Testament, hereby revoking any and all Wills and Codicils heretofore made by me.

FIRST: I direct that all my just debts and funeral expenses be paid out of my estate as soon after my death as is practicable.

SECOND: I give and bequeath the following personal property unto the following persons:

_____ to _____

_____ to _____

_____ to _____

THIRD: All the rest, residue and remainder of my estate, real or personal, wheresoever situate, now owned or hereafter acquired by me, which at the time of my death shall belong to me or be subject to my disposal by will, I give, devise and bequeath as follows:

_____% to my spouse, _____ and

_____% to my children, _____

_____

_____, in equal shares or to their lineal descendants per stirpes.

FOURTH: In the event that any beneficiary fails to survive me by thirty days, then this will shall take effect as if that person had predeceased me.

FIFTH: I hereby nominate, constitute and appoint _____ to serve as Executor of this, my Last Will and Testament, to serve without bond or surety. In the event that he or she is unable or unwilling to serve at any time or for any reason then I nominate, constitute and appoint _____ as alternate Executor also to serve without bond or surety. I give my said Executor the fullest power in all matters including the power to sell or convey real or personal property or any interest therein without court order. My Executor shall serve as an independent executor, and no action shall be had in the county court in relation to the settlement of my estate other than the probating and recording of my Will and the return of an inventory, appraisement and list of claims of my estate, as provided by law.

IN WITNESS WHEREOF I declare this to be my Last Will and Testament and execute it willingly as my free and voluntary act for the purposes expressed herein and I am of legal age and sound mind and make this under no constraint or undue influence, this _____ day of _____, _____.

_____

The foregoing instrument was on said date subscribed at the end thereof by _____, the above named Testator who signed, published, and declared this instrument to be his/her Last Will and Testament in the presence of us and each of us, who thereupon at his/her request, in his/her presence, and in the presence of each other, have hereunto subscribed our names as witnesses thereto. We understand this to be his/her will and to the best of our knowledge testator is of legal age, of sound mind and under no constraint or undue influence.

_____residing at_____

_____residing at_____

Last Will and Testament

I, _____ a resident of _____ County, Texas do hereby make, publish and declare this to be my Last Will and Testament, hereby revoking any and all Wills and Codicils heretofore made by me.

FIRST: I direct that all my just debts and funeral expenses be paid out of my estate as soon after my death as is practicable.

SECOND: I give and bequeath the following personal property unto the following persons:

_____ to _____

_____ to _____

_____ to _____

THIRD: All the rest, residue and remainder of my estate, real or personal, wheresoever situate, now owned or hereafter acquired by me, which at the time of my death shall belong to me or be subject to my disposal by will, I give, devise and bequeath unto my children _____

_____

_____,

plus any afterborn or adopted children in equal shares or to their lineal descendants per stirpes.

FOURTH: In the event that any beneficiary fails to survive me by thirty days, then this will shall take effect as if that person had predeceased me.

FIFTH: In the event any of my children have not attained the age of 18 years at the time of my death, I hereby nominate, constitute and appoint _____ as guardian over the person and estate of any of my children who have not reached the age of majority at the time of my death. In the event that said guardian is unable or unwilling to serve then I nominate, constitute and appoint _____ as guardian. Said guardian to serve without bond or surety.

SIXTH: I hereby nominate, constitute and appoint _____ to serve as Executor of this, my Last Will and Testament, to serve without bond or surety. In the event that he or she is unable or unwilling to serve at any time or for any reason then I nominate, constitute and appoint _____ as alternate Executor also to serve without bond or surety. I give my said Executor the fullest power in all matters including the power to sell or convey real or personal property or any interest therein without court order. My Executor shall serve as an independent executor, and no action shall be had in the county court in relation to the settlement of my estate other than the probating and recording of my Will and the return of an inventory, appraisement and list of claims of my estate, as provided by law.

IN WITNESS WHEREOF I declare this to be my Last Will and Testament and execute it willingly as my free and voluntary act for the purposes expressed herein and I am of legal age and sound mind and make this under no constraint or undue influence, this _____ day of _____, _____.

_____

The foregoing instrument was on said date subscribed at the end thereof by _____, the above named Testator who signed, published, and declared this instrument to be his/her Last Will and Testament in the presence of us and each of us, who thereupon at his/her request, in his/her presence, and in the presence of each other, have hereunto subscribed our names as witnesses thereto. We understand this to be his/her will and to the best of our knowledge testator is of legal age, of sound mind and under no constraint or undue influence.

_____residing at_____

_____residing at_____

Last Will and Testament

I, _____ a resident of _____ County, Texas do hereby make, publish and declare this to be my Last Will and Testament, hereby revoking any and all Wills and Codicils heretofore made by me.

FIRST: I direct that all my just debts and funeral expenses be paid out of my estate as soon after my death as is practicable.

SECOND: I give and bequeath the following personal property unto the following persons:

_____ to _____

_____ to _____

_____ to _____

THIRD: All the rest, residue and remainder of my estate, real or personal, wheresoever situate, now owned or hereafter acquired by me, which at the time of my death shall belong to me or be subject to my disposal by will, I give, devise and bequeath unto my children _____

_____

_____,

plus any afterborn or adopted children in equal shares or to their lineal descendants per stirpes.

FOURTH: In the event that any beneficiary fails to survive me by thirty days, then this will shall take effect as if that person had predeceased me.

FIFTH: In the event any of my children have not attained the age of 18 years at the time of my death, I hereby nominate, constitute and appoint _____ as guardian over the person of any of my children who have not reached the age of majority at the time of my death. In the event that said guardian is unable or unwilling to serve then I nominate, constitute and appoint _____ as guardian. Said guardian to serve without bond or surety.

SIXTH: In the event any of my children have not attained the age of 18 years at the time of my death, I hereby nominate, constitute and appoint _____ as guardian over the estate of any of my children who have not reached the age of majority at the time of my death. In the event that said guardian is unable or unwilling to serve then I nominate, constitute and appoint _____ as guardian. Said guardian to serve without bond or surety.

SEVENTH: I hereby nominate, constitute and appoint _____
to serve as Executor of this, my Last Will and Testament, to serve without bond or
surety. In the event that he or she is unable or unwilling to serve at any time or for any
reason then I nominate, constitute and appoint _____ as
alternate Executor also to serve without bond or surety. I give my said Executor the
fullest power in all matters including the power to sell or convey real or personal property or any interest therein without court order. My Executor shall serve as an
independent executor, and no action shall be had in the county court in relation to the
settlement of my estate other than the probating and recording of my Will and the
return of an inventory, appraisement and list of claims of my estate, as provided by law.

IN WITNESS WHEREOF I declare this to be my Last Will and Testament and
execute it willingly as my free and voluntary act for the purposes expressed herein and
I am of legal age and sound mind and make this under no constraint or undue influence,
this _____ day of _____, _____.

_____

The foregoing instrument was on said date subscribed at the end thereof by
_____, the above named Testator who signed,
published, and declared this instrument to be his/her Last Will and Testament in the
presence of us and each of us, who thereupon at his/her request, in his/her presence, and
in the presence of each other, have hereunto subscribed our names as witnesses thereto.
We understand this to be his/her will and to the best of our knowledge testator is of legal
age, of sound mind and under no constraint or undue influence.

_____residing at_____

_____residing at_____

Last Will and Testament

I, _____ a resident of _____ County, Texas do hereby make, publish and declare this to be my Last Will and Testament, hereby revoking any and all Wills and Codicils heretofore made by me.

FIRST: I direct that all my just debts and funeral expenses be paid out of my estate as soon after my death as is practicable.

SECOND: I give and bequeath the following personal property unto the following persons:

_____ to _____

_____ to _____

_____ to _____

THIRD: All the rest, residue and remainder of my estate, real or personal, wheresoever situate, now owned or hereafter acquired by me, which at the time of my death shall belong to me or be subject to my disposal by will, I give, devise and bequeath unto my children _____

_____

_____, plus any afterborn or adopted children in equal shares or to their lineal descendants per stirpes.

FOURTH: In the event that any beneficiary fails to survive me by thirty days, then this will shall take effect as if that person had predeceased me.

FIFTH: In the event that any of my children have not reached the age of _____ years at the time of my death, then the share of any such child shall be held IN TRUST by _____until such time as such child or children reach the age of _____ years. The trustee shall use the income and that part of the principal of the trust as is, in the discretion of the trustee, necessary or desirable to provide proper housing, medical care, food, clothing, entertainment and education for the trust beneficiaries. In the event the said trustee is unable or unwilling to serve for any reason, then I nominate, constitute and appoint _____ as alternate trustee. No bond shall be required of either trustee in any jurisdiction.

SIXTH: In the event any of my children have not attained the age of 18 years at the time of my death, I hereby nominate, constitute and appoint _____ as guardian over the property of any of my children who have not reached the age of majority at the time of my death. In the event that said guardian is unable or unwilling to serve then I nominate, constitute and appoint _____ as guardian. Said guardian to serve without bond or surety.

SEVENTH: I hereby nominate, constitute and appoint _____ to serve as Executor of this, my Last Will and Testament, to serve without bond or surety. In the event that he or she is unable or unwilling to serve at any time or for any reason then I nominate, constitute and appoint _____ as alternate Executor also to serve without bond or surety. I give my said Executor the fullest power in all matters including the power to sell or convey real or personal property or any interest therein without court order. My Executor shall serve as an independent executor, and no action shall be had in the county court in relation to the settlement of my estate other than the probating and recording of my Will and the return of an inventory, appraisement and list of claims of my estate, as provided by law.

IN WITNESS WHEREOF I declare this to be my Last Will and Testament and execute it willingly as my free and voluntary act for the purposes expressed herein and I am of legal age and sound mind and make this under no constraint or undue influence, this _____ day of _____, _____.

_____

The foregoing instrument was on said date subscribed at the end thereof by _____, the above named Testator who signed, published, and declared this instrument to be his/her Last Will and Testament in the presence of us and each of us, who thereupon at his/her request, in his/her presence, and in the presence of each other, have hereunto subscribed our names as witnesses thereto. We understand this to be his/her will and to the best of our knowledge testator is of legal age, of sound mind and under no constraint or undue influence.

_____residing at_____

_____residing at_____

Last Will and Testament

I, _____ a resident of _____ County, Texas do hereby make, publish and declare this to be my Last Will and Testament, hereby revoking any and all Wills and Codicils heretofore made by me.

FIRST: I direct that all my just debts and funeral expenses be paid out of my estate as soon after my death as is practicable.

SECOND: I give and bequeath the following personal property unto the following persons:

_____ to _____

_____ to _____

_____ to _____

THIRD: All the rest, residue and remainder of my estate, real or personal, wheresoever situate, now owned or hereafter acquired by me, which at the time of my death shall belong to me or be subject to my disposal by will, I give, devise and bequeath unto my children _____

_____

_____,

in equal shares, or their lineal descendants per stirpes.

FOURTH: In the event that any beneficiary fails to survive me by thirty days, then this will shall take effect as if that person had predeceased me.

FIFTH: I hereby nominate, constitute and appoint _____ to serve as Executor of this, my Last Will and Testament, to serve without bond or surety. In the event that he or she is unable or unwilling to serve at any time or for any reason then I nominate, constitute and appoint _____ as alternate Executor also to serve without bond or surety. I give my said Executor the fullest power in all matters including the power to sell or convey real or personal property or any interest therein without court order. My Executor shall serve as an independent executor, and no action shall be had in the county court in relation to the settlement of my estate other than the probating and recording of my Will and the return of an inventory, appraisement and list of claims of my estate, as provided by law.

    IN WITNESS WHEREOF I declare this to be my Last Will and Testament and execute it willingly as my free and voluntary act for the purposes expressed herein and I am of legal age and sound mind and make this under no constraint or undue influence, this _____ day of _____, _____.

_____

    The foregoing instrument was on said date subscribed at the end thereof by _____, the above named Testator who signed, published, and declared this instrument to be his/her Last Will and Testament in the presence of us and each of us, who thereupon at his/her request, in his/her presence, and in the presence of each other, have hereunto subscribed our names as witnesses thereto. We understand this to be his/her will and to the best of our knowledge testator is of legal age, of sound mind and under no constraint or undue influence.

_____residing at_____

_____residing at_____

Last Will and Testament

I, _____ a resident of _____ County, Texas do hereby make, publish and declare this to be my Last Will and Testament, hereby revoking any and all Wills and Codicils heretofore made by me.

FIRST: I direct that all my just debts and funeral expenses be paid out of my estate as soon after my death as is practicable.

SECOND: I give and bequeath the following personal property unto the following persons:

_____ to _____

_____ to _____

_____ to _____

THIRD: All the rest, residue and remainder of my estate, real or personal, wheresoever situate, now owned or hereafter acquired by me, which at the time of my death shall belong to me or be subject to my disposal by will, I give, devise and bequeath unto my children _____

_____

_____,

in equal shares, or their lineal descendants per capita.

FOURTH: In the event that any beneficiary fails to survive me by thirty days, then this will shall take effect as if that person had predeceased me.

FIFTH: I hereby nominate, constitute and appoint _____ to serve as Executor of this, my Last Will and Testament, to serve without bond or surety. In the event that he or she is unable or unwilling to serve at any time or for any reason then I nominate, constitute and appoint _____ as alternate Executor also to serve without bond or surety. I give my said Executor the fullest power in all matters including the power to sell or convey real or personal property or any interest therein without court order. My Executor shall serve as an independent executor, and no action shall be had in the county court in relation to the settlement of my estate other than the probating and recording of my Will and the return of an inventory, appraisement and list of claims of my estate, as provided by law.

IN WITNESS WHEREOF I declare this to be my Last Will and Testament and execute it willingly as my free and voluntary act for the purposes expressed herein and I am of legal age and sound mind and make this under no constraint or undue influence, this _____ day of _____, _____.

_____

The foregoing instrument was on said date subscribed at the end thereof by _____, the above named Testator who signed, published, and declared this instrument to be his/her Last Will and Testament in the presence of us and each of us, who thereupon at his/her request, in his/her presence, and in the presence of each other, have hereunto subscribed our names as witnesses thereto. We understand this to be his/her will and to the best of our knowledge testator is of legal age, of sound mind and under no constraint or undue influence.

_____residing at_____

_____residing at_____

Last Will and Testament

I, _____ a resident of _____ County, Texas do hereby make, publish and declare this to be my Last Will and Testament, hereby revoking any and all Wills and Codicils heretofore made by me.

FIRST: I direct that all my just debts and funeral expenses be paid out of my estate as soon after my death as is practicable.

SECOND: I give and bequeath the following personal property unto the following persons:

_____ to _____

_____ to _____

_____ to _____

THIRD: All the rest, residue and remainder of my estate, real or personal, wheresoever situate, now owned or hereafter acquired by me, which at the time of my death shall belong to me or be subject to my disposal by will, I give, devise and bequeath unto the following: _____

_____

_____

_____, or to the survivor of them.

FOURTH: In the event that any beneficiary fails to survive me by thirty days, then this will shall take effect as if that person had predeceased me.

FIFTH: I hereby nominate, constitute and appoint _____ to serve as Executor of this, my Last Will and Testament, to serve without bond or surety. In the event that he or she is unable or unwilling to serve at any time or for any reason then I nominate, constitute and appoint _____ as alternate Executor also to serve without bond or surety. I give my said Executor the fullest power in all matters including the power to sell or convey real or personal property or any interest therein without court order. My Executor shall serve as an independent executor, and no action shall be had in the county court in relation to the settlement of my estate other than the probating and recording of my Will and the return of an inventory, appraisement and list of claims of my estate, as provided by law.

IN WITNESS WHEREOF I declare this to be my Last Will and Testament and execute it willingly as my free and voluntary act for the purposes expressed herein and I am of legal age and sound mind and make this under no constraint or undue influence, this _____ day of _____, _____.

_____

The foregoing instrument was on said date subscribed at the end thereof by _____, the above named Testator who signed, published, and declared this instrument to be his/her Last Will and Testament in the presence of us and each of us, who thereupon at his/her request, in his/her presence, and in the presence of each other, have hereunto subscribed our names as witnesses thereto. We understand this to be his/her will and to the best of our knowledge testator is of legal age, of sound mind and under no constraint or undue influence.

_____residing at_____

_____residing at_____

Last Will and Testament

I, _____ a resident of _____ County, Texas do hereby make, publish and declare this to be my Last Will and Testament, hereby revoking any and all Wills and Codicils heretofore made by me.

FIRST: I direct that all my just debts and funeral expenses be paid out of my estate as soon after my death as is practicable.

SECOND: I give and bequeath the following personal property unto the following persons:

_____ to _____

_____ to _____

_____ to _____

THIRD: All the rest, residue and remainder of my estate, real or personal, wheresoever situate, now owned or hereafter acquired by me, which at the time of my death shall belong to me or be subject to my disposal by will, I give, devise and bequeath unto the following _____

_____

_____,

in equal shares, or their lineal descendants per stirpes.

FOURTH: In the event that any beneficiary fails to survive me by thirty days, then this will shall take effect as if that person had predeceased me.

FIFTH: I hereby nominate, constitute and appoint _____ to serve as Executor of this, my Last Will and Testament, to serve without bond or surety. In the event that he or she is unable or unwilling to serve at any time or for any reason then I nominate, constitute and appoint _____ as alternate Executor also to serve without bond or surety. I give my said Executor the fullest power in all matters including the power to sell or convey real or personal property or any interest therein without court order. My Executor shall serve as an independent executor, and no action shall be had in the county court in relation to the settlement of my estate other than the probating and recording of my Will and the return of an inventory, appraisement and list of claims of my estate, as provided by law.

IN WITNESS WHEREOF I declare this to be my Last Will and Testament and execute it willingly as my free and voluntary act for the purposes expressed herein and I am of legal age and sound mind and make this under no constraint or undue influence, this _____ day of _____, _____.

_____

The foregoing instrument was on said date subscribed at the end thereof by _____, the above named Testator who signed, published, and declared this instrument to be his/her Last Will and Testament in the presence of us and each of us, who thereupon at his/her request, in his/her presence, and in the presence of each other, have hereunto subscribed our names as witnesses thereto. We understand this to be his/her will and to the best of our knowledge testator is of legal age, of sound mind and under no constraint or undue influence.

_____residing at_____

_____residing at_____

Self-Proving Affidavit

STATE OF TEXAS   §
                                                  §
COUNTY OF _____   §

      BEFORE ME, the undersigned authority, on this day personally appeared _____, _____ and _____, known to me to be the Testator and the witnesses, respectively, whose names are subscribed to the annexed or foregoing instrument in their respective capacities; and all of said persons being by me duly sworn, the Testator declared to me and to the witnesses in my presence that said instrument is his/her Will, and that he/she had willingly made and executed it as his/her free act and deed for the purposes therein expressed; and the witnesses, each on his oath, stated to me in the presence and hearing of the Testator that the Testator had declared to them that said instrument is his/her Will, and that he/she executed same as such and wanted each of them to sign it as a witness; and upon their oaths each witness stated further that they did sign the same as witnesses in the presence of the Testator and at his/her request, that he/she was at that time eighteen (18) years of age or over and was of sound mind, and that each of the witnesses was then at least fourteen (14) years of age.

_____
TESTATOR

_____
WITNESS

_____
WITNESS

SUBSCRIBED AND ACKNOWLEDGED before me by _____, the Testator and subscribed and sworn to before me by the above-named witnesses this _____ day of _____, _____.

_____
Notary Public

_____
[Print Name]
State of Texas
My Commission Expires: _____

Page _____ of _____

This page intentionally blank.

First Codicil to the Will of

_____

I, _____, a resident of _____ County, Texas declare this to be the first codicil to my Last Will and Testament dated _____, _____.

FIRST: I hereby revoke the clause of my Will which reads as follows: _____
_____
_____
_____

SECOND: I hereby add following clause to my Will: _____
_____
_____
_____

THIRD: In all other respects I hereby confirm and republish my Last Will and Testament dated _____, _____.

Date: _____   _____

We, the undersigned persons, of lawful age, have on this _____ day of _____, _____, at the request of _____, witnessed his/her signature to the foregoing First Codicil to Will in the presence of each of us; and we have, at the same time and in his/her presence and in the presence of each other, subscribed our names hereto as attesting witnesses.

_____ residing at: _____
                                                _____
_____ residing at: _____
                                                _____

SELF-PROVING AFFIDAVIT

STATE OF TEXAS   §
                                   §
COUNTY OF _____   §

BEFORE ME, the undersigned authority, on this day personally appeared _____, _____, and_____, known to me to be the Testator and the witnesses, respectively, whose names are subscribed to the annexed or foregoing instrument in their respective capacities; and all of said persons being by me duly sworn, the Testator declared to me and to the witnesses in my presence that said instrument is his/her First Codicil to Will, and that he/she had willingly made and executed it as his/her free act and deed for the purposes therein expressed; and the witnesses, each on his oath, stated to me in the presence and hearing of the Testator that the Testator had declared to them that said instrument is his/her First Codicil to Will, and that he/she executed same as such and wanted each of them to sign it as a witness; and upon their oaths each witness stated further that they did sign the same as witnesses in the presence of the Testator and at his/her request, that he/she was at that time eighteen (18) years of age or over and was of sound mind, and that each of the witnesses was then at least fourteen (14) years of age.

_____   _____
TESTATOR   WITNESS

                                         _____
                                         WITNESS

SUBSCRIBED AND ACKNOWLEDGED before me by _____, the Testator and subscribed and sworn to before me by the above-named witnesses this _____ day of _____, _____.

                                         _____
                                         Notary Public

                                         Page _____ of _____

This page intentionally blank.

DIRECTIVE TO PHYSICIANS AND
FAMILY OR SURROGATES

This is an important legal document known as an Advance Directive. It is designed to help you communicate your wishes about medical treatment at some time in the future when you are unable to make your wishes known because of illness or injury. These wishes are usually based on personal values. In particular, you may want to consider what burdens or hardships of treatment you would be willing to accept for a particular amount of benefit obtained if you were seriously ill.

You are encouraged to discuss your values and wishes with your family or chosen spokesperson, as well as your physician. Your physician, other health care provider, or medical institution may provide you with various resources to assist you in completing your advance directive. Brief definitions are listed within the document and may aid you in your discussions and advance planning. Initial the treatment choices that best reflect your personal preferences. Provide a copy of your directive to your physician, usual hospital, and family or spokesperson. Consider a periodic review of this document. By periodic review, you can best assure that the directive reflects your preferences.

In addition to this advance directive, Texas law provides for two other types of directives that can be important during a serious illness. These are the Medical Power of Attorney and the Out-of-Hospital Do-Not-Resuscitate Order. You may wish to discuss these with your physician, family, hospital representative, or other advisers. You may also wish to complete a directive related to the donation of organs and tissues.

DEFINITIONS:

"Artificial nutrition and hydration" means the provision of nutrients or fluids by a tube inserted in a vein, under the skin in the subcutaneous tissues, or in the stomach (gastrointestinal tract).

"Irreversible condition" means a condition, injury, or illness: that may be treated, but is never cured or eliminated that leaves a person unable to care for or make decisions for the person's own self; and that, without life-sustaining treatment provided in accordance with the prevailing standard of medical care, is fatal.

Explanation: Many serious illnesses such as cancer, failure of major organs (kidney, heart, liver, or lung), and serious brain disease such as Alzheimer's dementia may be considered irreversible early on. There is no cure, but the patient may be kept alive for prolonged periods of time if the patient receives life-sustaining treatments. Late in the course of the same illness, the disease may be considered terminal when, even with treatment, the patient is expected to die. You may wish to consider which burdens of treatment you would be willing to accept in an effort to achieve a particular outcome.

Page _____ of _____

This is a very personal decision that you may wish to discuss with your physician, family, or other important persons in your life.

"Life-sustaining treatment" means treatment that, based on reasonable medical judgment, sustains the life of a patient without which the patient will die. The term includes both life-sustaining medications and artificial life support such as mechanical breathing machines, kidney dialysis treatment, and artificial hydration and nutrition. The term does not include the administration of pain management medication, the performance of a medical procedure necessary to provide comfort care, or any other medical care provided to alleviate a patient's pain.

"Terminal condition" means an incurable condition caused by injury, disease, or illness that according to reasonable medical judgment will produce death within six months, even with available life-sustaining treatment provided in accordance with the prevailing standard of medical care.

Explanation: Many serious illnesses may be considered irreversible early in the course of the illness, but they may not be considered terminal until the disease is fairly advanced. In thinking about terminal illness and its treatment, you may wish to consider the relative benefits and burdens of treatment and discuss your wishes with your physician, family, or other important persons in your life.

Page _____ of _____

Advance Directive

I, _____, recognize that the best health care is based upon a partnership of trust and communication with my physician. My physician and I will make health care decisions together as long as I am of sound mind and able to make my wishes known. If there comes a time that I am unable to make medical decisions about myself because of illness or injury, I direct that the following treatment preferences be honored:

'   If, in the judgment of my physician, I am suffering with a terminal condition from which I am expected to die within six months, even with available life-sustaining treatment provided in accordance with prevailing standards of medical care:

_____   I request that all treatments other than those needed to keep me comfortable be discontinued or withheld and my physician allow me to die as gently as possible; OR

_____   I request that I be kept alive in this terminal condition using available life-sustaining treatment. (THIS SELECTION DOES NOT APPLY TO HOSPICE CARE.)

        If, in the judgment of my physician, I am suffering with an irreversible condition so that I cannot care for myself or make decisions for myself and am expected to die without life-sustaining treatment provided in accordance with prevailing standards of medical care:

_____   I request that all treatment other than those needed to keep me comfortable be discontinued or withheld and my physician allow me to die as gently as possible;
        OR

_____   I request that I be kept alive in this irreversible condition using available life-sustaining treatment. (THIS SELECTION DOES NOT APPLY TO HOSPICE CARE.)

        Additional requests: (After discussion with your physician, you may wish to consider listing particular treatments in this space that you do or do not want in specific circumstances, such as artificial nutrition and fluids, intravenous antibiotics, etc. Be sure to state whether you do or do not want the particular treatment.)

_____

_____

        After signing this directive, if my representative or I elect hospice care, I understand and agree that only those treatments needed to keep me comfortable would be provided and I would not be given available life-sustaining treatments.

        If I do not have a Medical Power of Attorney, and I am unable to make my wishes known, I designate the following person(s) to make treatment decisions with my physician compatible with my personal values:

        1. _____
        2. _____

        (If a Medical Power of Attorney has been executed, than an agent already has been named and you should not list additional names in this document.)

If the above persons are not available, or if I have not designated a spokesperson, I understand that a **spokesperson** will be chosen for me following standards specified in the laws of Texas. If, in the judgment of my physician, my death is imminent within minutes to hours, even with the use of all available medical treatment provided within the prevailing standard of care, I acknowledge that all treatments may be withheld or removed except those needed to maintain my comfort. I understand that under Texas law this directive has no effect if I have been diagnosed as pregnant. This directive will remain in effect until I revoke it. No other person may do so.

Signed this _____ day of _____ , _____, in _____ , _____ County, Texas.

_____

[Print Name]: _____

The witnesses acknowledge that the declarant signed this directive in their presence and that each of them is over the age of eighteen (18) years and competent to witness this document. The witness designated at "Witness 1" is: (1) not a person designated by the declarant to make a treatment decision for the declarant; (2) not related to the declarant by blood or marriage; (3) not entitled to any portion of the declarant's estate on declarant's death; (4) not a claimant against the estate of the declarant; (5) not the attending physician or employee of the attending physician of declarant; and (6) not an officer, director, partner, or business office employee of a health care facility in which the declarant is being cared for or of any parent organization of the health care facility. Furthermore, if "Witness 1" is an employee of a health care facility in which the declarant is a patient, such witness is not involved in providing direct patient care to the declarant.

_____
Witness 1
Address: _____
_____

_____
Witness 2
Address: _____
_____

INFORMATION CONCERNING THE
MEDICAL POWER OF ATTORNEY

THIS IS AN IMPORTANT LEGAL DOCUMENT. BEFORE SIGNING THIS DOCUMENT, YOU SHOULD KNOW THESE IMPORTANT FACTS:

Except to the extent you state otherwise, this document gives the person you name as your agent the authority to make any and all health care decisions for you in accordance with your wishes, including your religious and moral beliefs, when you are no longer capable of making them yourself. Because "health care" means any treatment, service, or procedure to maintain, diagnose, or treat your physical or mental condition, your agent has the power to make a broad range of health care decisions for you. Your agent may consent, refuse to consent, or withdraw consent to medical treatment and may make decisions about withdrawing or withholding life-sustaining treatment. Your agent may not consent to voluntary inpatient mental health services, convulsive treatment, psychosurgery, or abortion. A physician must comply with your agent's instructions or allow you to be transferred to another physician.

Your agent's authority begins when your doctor certifies that you lack the capacity to make health care decisions.

Your agent is obligated to follow your instructions when making decisions on your behalf. Unless you state otherwise, your agent has the same authority to make decisions about your health care as you would have had.

It is important that you discuss this document with your physician or other health care provider before you sign it to make sure that you understand the nature and range of decisions that may be made on your behalf. If you do not have a physician, you should talk with someone else who is knowledgeable about these issues and can answer your questions. You do not need a lawyer's assistance to complete this document, but if there is anything in this document that you do not understand, you should ask a lawyer to explain it to you.

The person you appoint as agent should be someone you know and trust. The person must be 18 years of age or older or a person under 18 years of age who has had the disabilities of minority removed. If you appoint your health or residential care provider (e.g., your physician or an employee of a home health agency, hospital, nursing home, or residential care home, other than a relative), that person has to choose between acting as your agent or as your health or residential care provider; the law does not permit a person to do both at the same time.

You should inform the person you appoint that you want the person to be your health care agent. You should discuss this document with your agent and your physician and give each a signed copy. You should indicate on the document itself the people and institutions who have signed copies. Your agent is not liable for health care decisions made in good faith on your behalf.

Page _____ of _____

Even after you have signed this document, you have the right to make health care decisions for yourself as long as you are able to do so and treatment cannot be given to you or stopped over your objection. You have the right to revoke the authority granted to your agent by informing your agent or your health or residential care provider orally or in writing, or by your execution of a subsequent Medical Power of Attorney. Unless you state otherwise, your appointment of a spouse dissolves on divorce.

This document may not be changed or modified. If you want to make changes in the document, you must make an entirely new one.

You may wish to designate an alternate agent in the event that your agent is unwilling, unable, or ineligible to act as your agent. Any alternate agent you designate has the same authority to make health care decisions for you.

THIS POWER OF ATTORNEY IS NOT VALID UNLESS IT IS SIGNED IN THE PRESENCE OF TWO OR MORE COMPETENT ADULT WITNESSES. THE FOLLOWING PERSONS MAY NOT ACT AS ONE OF THE WITNESSES:

(1)   the person you have designed as your agent;

(2)   a person related to you by blood or marriage;

(3)   a person entitled to any part of your estate after your death under a will or codicil executed by you or by operation of law;

(4)   your attending physician;

(5)   an employee of your attending physician;

(6)   an employee of a health care facility in which you are a patient if the employee is providing direct patient care to you or is an officer, director, partner, or business office employee of the health care facility or of any parent organization of the health care facility; or

(7)   a person who, at the time this power of attorney is executed, has a claim against any part of your estate after your death.

MEDICAL POWER OF ATTORNEY
AND DESIGNATION OF HEALTH CARE AGENT

1. DESIGNATION OF HEALTH CARE AGENT

I, _____, appoint:

Name: _____

Address: _____

_____

Phone: _____

as my agent to make any and all health care decisions for me, except to the extent I state otherwise in this document. This Medical Power of Attorney takes effect if I become unable to make my own health care decisions and this fact is certified in writing by my physician.

LIMITATIONS ON THE DECISION MAKING AUTHORITY OF MY AGENT ARE AS FOLLOWS:

_____

_____

2. DESIGNATION OF ALTERNATE AGENT

(You are not required to designate an alternate agent but you may do so. An alternate agent may make the same health care decisions as the designated agent if the designated agent is unable or unwilling to act as your agent. If the agent designated is your spouse, the designation is automatically revoked by law if your marriage is dissolved).

If the person designated as my agent is unable or unwilling to make health care decisions for me, I designate the following person to serve as my agent to make health care decisions for me as authorized by this document:

First Alternate Agent

Name: _____

Address: _____

_____

Phone: _____

Second Alternate Agent

Name: _____

Address: _____

_____

Phone: _____

An original of this document is kept at:

_____

_____

The following individuals or institutions have signed copies:

Name: _____

Address: _____

_____

Phone: _____

Name: _____

Address: _____

_____

Phone: _____

3.   DURATION

I understand that this Medical Power of Attorney exists indefinitely from the date I execute this document unless I establish a shorter time or revoke the power of attorney. If I am unable to make health care decisions for myself when this power of attorney expires, the authority I have granted my agent continues to exist until the time I become able to make health care decisions for myself.

(IF APPLICABLE) This Medical Power of Attorney ends on the following date:

_____

4.   PRIOR DESIGNATIONS REVOKED

I revoke any prior Medical Power of Attorney.

5. ACKNOWLEDGMENT OF DISCLOSURE STATEMENT

I have been provided with a disclosure statement explaining the effect of this document. I have read and understand that information contained in the disclosure statement.

(YOU MUST DATE AND SIGN THIS POWER OF ATTORNEY.)

I sign my name to this Medical Power of Attorney on the _____ day of _____, 20 _____ , at _____, _____ County, Texas.

_____

Print Name: _____

STATEMENT AND SIGNATURE OF FIRST WITNESS:

I am not the person appointed as agent by this document. I am not related to the principal by blood or marriage. I would not be entitled to any portion of the principal's estate on the principal's death. I am not the attending physician of the principal or an employee of the attending physician. I have no claim against any portion of the principals estate on the principal's death. Furthermore, if I am an employee of a health care facility in which the principal is a patient, I am not involved in providing direct patient care to the principal and am not an officer, director, partner, or business office employee of the health care facility or of any parent organization of the health care facility.

Witness Signature: _____

Print Name: _____ Date: _____

Address: _____

SIGNATURE OF SECOND WITNESS:

Witness Signature: _____

Print Name: _____ Date: _____

Address: _____

This page intentionally blank.

DECLARATION OF GUARDIAN IN THE EVENT
OF LATER INCAPACITY OR NEED OF GUARDIAN

I, _____, make this Declaration of Guardian, to operate if the need for a guardian for me later arises.

1. I designate _____ to serve as a guardian of my person, _____ as first alternate guardian of my person, _____ as second alternate guardian of my person, and _____ as third alternate guardian of my person.

2. I designate _____ to serve as guardian of my estate, _____ as first alternate guardian of my estate, _____ as second alternate guardian of my estate, and _____ as third alternate guardian of my estate.

3. If any guardian or alternate guardian dies, does not qualify, or resigns, the next named alternate guardian becomes my guardian.

4. I expressly disqualify the following person(s) from serving as guardian of my person: _____.

5. I expressly disqualify the following person(s) from serving as guardian of my estate: _____.

SIGNED this _____ day of _____, 20_____.

Witness _____   Print Name: _____

Witness _____   Print Name: _____

SELF-PROVING AFFIDAVIT

STATE OF TEXAS   §

                                   §

COUNTY OF _____ §

BEFORE ME, the undersigned authority, on this date personally appeared _____, _____ and _____, the declarant and witnesses, respectively, and all being duly sworn, the declarant said that the above instrument was his or her Declaration of Guardian and that the declarant had made and executed it for the purposes expressed in the declaration. The witnesses declared to me that they are each 14 years of age or older, that they saw the declarant sign the declaration, that they signed the declaration as witnesses, and that the declarant appeared to them to be of sound mind.

Declarant _____

Witness _____

Witness _____

SUBSCRIBED AND SWORN to before me by the above named declarant and witnesses on this the _____ day of _____, 20_____.

Name [print]: _____
Notary Public, State of Texas
My commission expires: _____

DECLARATION OF APPOINTMENT OF GUARDIAN
FOR MY CHILDREN IN THE EVENT OF MY DEATH OR INCAPACITY

I, _____, make this Declaration to appoint as guardian my child or children, listed herein, in the event of my death or incapacity:

Child: _____

Birthdate: _____

Child: _____

Birthdate: _____

I designate _____ to serve as guardian of the person of my (child or children), _____ as first alternate guardian of the person of my (child or children), _____ as second alternate guardian of the person of my (child or children), and _____ as third alternate guardian of the person of my (child or children).

I direct that the guardian of the person of my (child or children) serve (with or without) bond.

I designate _____ to serve as guardian of the estate of my (child or children), _____ as first alternate guardian of the estate of my (child or children), _____ as second alternate guardian of the estate of my (child or children), and _____ as third alternate guardian of the estate of my (child or children).

If any guardian or alternate guardian dies, does not qualify, or resigns the next named alternate guardian becomes guardian of my (child or children).

Signed this _____ day of _____, 20_____.

Declarant _____
Print Name: _____

Witness _____

Witness _____

Page _____ of _____

SELF-PROVING AFFIDAVIT

STATE OF TEXAS §

§

COUNTY OF _____ §

BEFORE ME, the undersigned authority, on this date personally appeared _____, _____ and _____, as witnesses, and all being duly sworn, the declarant said that the above instrument was his or her Declaration of Appointment of Guardian for the Declarant's Children in the Event of Declarant's Death or Incapacity and that declarant had made and executed it for the purposes expressed in the declaration. The witnesses declared to me that they are each 14 years of age or older, that they saw the declarant sign the declaration, that they signed the declaration as witnesses, and that the declarant appeared to them to be of sound mind.

Declarant: _____

Witness: _____

Witness: _____

Subscribed and sworn to before me by the above named declarant and affiants on this _____ day of _____, 20_____.

Name [Print]: _____
Notary Public, State of Texas
My commission expires: _____

Page _____ of _____

AUTHORIZATION TO CONSENT TO MEDICAL TREATMENT

We, _____ and _____, of
_____, City of _____, _____,
County, State of _____, are the biological parents and managing conserva-
tors of the following minor child(ren): _____
_____

Pursuant to Texas Family Code §35.01(a), we authorize _____ and/or
_____ in whose care such child(ren) have been entrusted from time to
time with our permission, to consent to any X-ray examination, anesthetic, medical or
surgical diagnosis or treatment, and hospital care, to be rendered to the child(ren) under
the general or special supervision and on the advice of any physician or surgeon licensed
to practice medicine, and to consent to any X-ray examination, anesthetic, dental or surgical diagnosis or treatment, and hospital care to be rendered to the child(ren) by any
dentist licensed to practice dentistry.

Dated:_____, 20____   _____
                                                  Name of Parent

                                                  _____
                                                  Name of Parent

STATE OF TEXAS   )

COUNTY OF _____   )

    Subscribed, sworn to and acknowledged before me by _____
and _____ this _____ day of _____, 20___.

                                    _____
                                    Notary Public, State of Texas
                                    My commission expires:_____

This page intentionally blank.

AUTHORIZATION TO CONSENT TO MEDICAL TREATMENT

I, _____, of _____, City of

_____, _____, County, State of _____, am the

biological parent and sole managing conservator of the following minor child(ren):

_____

_____

Pursuant to Texas Family Code §35.01(a), I authorize _____ and/or

_____ in whose care such child(ren) have been entrusted from

_____, 20_____ through _____, 20_____, to consent to any X-ray

examination, anesthetic, medical or surgical diagnosis or treatment, and hospital care,

to be rendered to the child(ren) under the general or special supervision and on the

advice of any physician or surgeon licensed to practice medicine, and to consent to any

X-ray examination, anesthetic, dental or surgical diagnosis or treatment, and hospital

care to be rendered to the child(ren) by any dentist licensed to practice dentistry.

Dated:_____, 20_____   _____
                                                Name of Parent

STATE OF TEXAS   )
)
COUNTY OF _____   )

    Subscribed, sworn to and acknowledged before me by _____

this _____ day of _____, 20_____.

_____

Notary Public, State of Texas

My commission expires:_____

This page intentionally blank.

UNIFORM DONOR CARD

The undersigned hereby makes this anatomical gift, if medically acceptable, to take effect on death. The words and marks below indicate my desires:

I give:

(a) ____ any needed organs or parts;

(b) ____ only the following organs or parts

_____

for the purpose of transplantation, therapy, medical research, or education;

(c) ____ my body for anatomical study if needed.

Limitations or special wishes, if any:

_____

Signed by the donor and the following witnesses in the presence of each other:

_____   _____
Signature of Donor   Date of birth

_____   _____
Date signed   City & State

_____   _____
Witness   Witness

_____   _____
Address   Address

UNIFORM DONOR CARD

The undersigned hereby makes this anatomical gift, if medically acceptable, to take effect on death. The words and marks below indicate my desires:

I give:

(a) ____ any needed organs or parts;

(b) ____ only the following organs or parts

_____

for the purpose of transplantation, therapy, medical research, or education;

(c) ____ my body for anatomical study if needed.

Limitations or special wishes, if any:

_____

Signed by the donor and the following witnesses in the presence of each other:

_____   _____
Signature of Donor   Date of birth

_____   _____
Date signed   City & State

_____   _____
Witness   Witness

_____   _____
Address   Address

UNIFORM DONOR CARD

The undersigned hereby makes this anatomical gift, if medically acceptable, to take effect on death. The words and marks below indicate my desires:

I give:

(a) ____ any needed organs or parts;

(b) ____ only the following organs or parts

_____

for the purpose of transplantation, therapy, medical research, or education;

(c) ____ my body for anatomical study if needed.

Limitations or special wishes, if any:

_____

Signed by the donor and the following witnesses in the presence of each other:

_____   _____
Signature of Donor   Date of birth

_____   _____
Date signed   City & State

_____   _____
Witness   Witness

_____   _____
Address   Address

UNIFORM DONOR CARD

The undersigned hereby makes this anatomical gift, if medically acceptable, to take effect on death. The words and marks below indicate my desires:

I give:

(a) ____ any needed organs or parts;

(b) ____ only the following organs or parts

_____

for the purpose of transplantation, therapy, medical research, or education;

(c) ____ my body for anatomical study if needed.

Limitations or special wishes, if any:

_____

Signed by the donor and the following witnesses in the presence of each other:

_____   _____
Signature of Donor   Date of birth

_____   _____
Date signed   City & State

_____   _____
Witness   Witness

_____   _____
Address   Address

One of these cards should be cut out and carried in your wallet or purse.

Index

U

unified credit, 20, 25, 26
uniform donor card, 61

V

validity, 1, 22, 23, 39, 40, 45, 46, 56

W

witnesses, 22, 23, 34, 39, 40, 41, 45, 46, 53,
    55, 56, 61

How to Use the CD-ROM

Thank you for purchasing *Write Your Own Texas Will (+CD-ROM)*. We have included every document in the book on the CD-ROM that is attached to the inside back cover of the book.

You can use these forms just as you would the forms in the book. Print them out, fill them in, and use them however you need. You can also fill in the forms directly on your computer. Just identify the form you need, open it, click on the space where the information should go, and input your information. Customize each form for your particular needs. Use them over and over again.

The CD-ROM is compatible with both PC and Mac operating systems. (While it should work with either operating system, we cannot guarantee that it will work with your particular system and we cannot provide technical assistance.) To use the forms on your computer, you will need to use Adobe® Reader®. The CD-ROM does not contain this program. You can download this program from Adobe's website at **www.adobe.com**. Click on the "Get Adobe® Reader®" icon to begin the download process and follow the instructions.

Once you have Adobe® Reader® installed, insert the CD-ROM into your computer. Double click on the icon representing the disc on your desktop or go through your hard drive to identify the drive that contains the disc and click on it.

Once opened, you will see the files contained on the CD-ROM listed as "Form #: [Form Title]." Open the file you need through Adobe® Reader®. You may print the form to fill it out manually at this point, or your can use the "Hand Tool" and click on the appropriate line to fill it in using your computer.

Any time you see bracketed information [ ] on the form, you can click on it and delete the bracketed information from your final form. This information is only a reference guide to assist you in filling in the forms and should be removed from your final version. Once all your information is filled in, you can print your filled-in form.

NOTE: *Adobe® Reader® does not allow you to save the PDF with the boxes filled in.*

• • • • •

Purchasers of this book are granted a license to use the forms contained in it for their own personal use. By purchasing this book, you have also purchased a limited license to use all forms on the accompanying CD-ROM. The license limits you to personal use only and all other copyright laws must be adhered. No claim of copyright is made in any government form reproduced in the book or on the CD-ROM. You are free to modify the forms and tailor them to your specific situation.

The author and publisher have attempted to provide the most current and up-to-date information available. However, the courts, Congress, and your state's legislatures review, modify, and change laws on an ongoing basis, as well as create new laws from time to time. By the very nature of the information and due to the continual changes in our legal system, to be sure that you have the current and best information for your situation, you should consult a local attorney or research the current laws yourself.

• • • • •